G. K. CHESTERTON: EXPLORATIONS IN ALLEGORY

G. K. CHESTERTON: EXPLORATIONS IN ALLEGORY

LYNETTE HUNTER

St. Martin's Press　New York

All rights reserved. For information, write:
St. Martin's Press, Inc. 175 Fifth Avenue, New York, NY 10010
Printed in Great Britain
First published in the United States of America in 1979

ISBN 0–312–31492–2

Library of Congress Cataloging in Publication Data

Hunter, Lynette.
    G. K. Chesterton: explorations in allegory.

    Includes bibliographical references and index.
    1. Chesterton, Gilbert Keith, 1874–1936–Criticism
and interpretation. 2. Allegory.
PR4453.C4Z654   1979   828'.9'1209   79–4643
ISBN 0–312–31492–2

To Peter Lichtenfels

Contents

1 Early Landscapes

G. K. Chesterton says at the beginning of his *Autobiography* that his first memory was of 'a young man walking across a bridge . . . he carried in his hand a disproportionately large key of a shining yellow metal and wore a large golden or gilded crown'. As he himself realised the image was a summation of the explorations of his life. It reflected the sense of immanent danger on either side of the bridge and the possibility of achieving an understanding of his life if he could only cross the bridge.

Chesterton was born in 1874 and by the late 1880s he had already begun looking around him for the keys to unlock the mystery of the world. But from the first he felt surrounded by philosophies that lacked substance. He vividly remembers seeming to have only two choices; materialism with its didactic and rationalistic approach to mankind, or aestheticism with its depths of pessimism. Both philosophies and their attendant artistic expression carried for Chesterton the assumption of absolute human creativity which he instinctively felt to be personally destructive yet dangerously close. His fears prompted him to set off early in pursuit of an external authority and a style in which to express both this authority and his own identity.

Chesterton tells us in his *Autobiography* that by the time he left school he had already refused to accept the purely rationalistic view that drained the world of 'wonder'. In the face of the surrounding materialism he turned to painting and in 1892 he entered the Slade School of Art. Yet his experience of the dominant impressionist school of art was a strong sense of flux, which, by all accounts, had an even stronger effect on him. He came to refer to the effect as solipsism, his madness, his lunacy, his constant fear. It did not take him long to turn to a form of personal religion to provide the necessary stability for his life. In *Autobiography* he says:

> At a very early age I had thought my way back to thought itself. It is a very dreadful thing to do; for it may lead to thinking that there is nothing but thought.[1]

1

Not until 1908, when he wrote *Orthodoxy*, did he find in the Anglican Church the 'thought that stops thought'. But in the 1890s, coming from an Unitarian home, he was not yet interested in organised religion and seemed to have a choice only between the ideological streams of rationalism and impressionism. As a result he was faced with the dilemma of depriving his vision of life of wonder or going mad. The young Chesterton set about to find a compromise, to explore and experiment with many different styles hoping to find one with which to communicate his individual vision.

Chesterton is reticent in his *Autobiography* about the exact details of the fear in the part of his life which he spent at the Slade, thereby leaving it open to any interpretation. Various biographers point us in the direction of sexual sadism, satanism or homosexuality.[2] But two books contemporaneous with *Autobiography*, *Robert Louis Stevenson* and *The Poet and the Lunatics*, describe a similar fear in much greater detail. They contain many direct insights into his own early life that Chesterton could not voice in his autobiography.

The study of Stevenson among the 'pessimists and nihilists' of Paris is probably an account of Chesterton's own feelings in the nineties, but the similarity between the two men goes further back than this. Stevenson is described as being deeply affected by the change from boyhood into youth. Chesterton suggests that it was the shock of Stevenson's abrupt plunge into adult life that turned him back to the pleasures of childhood; it was similar to the escape from the 'morbidity' of Chesterton's own youth that is mentioned in *Autobiography*. The exact nature of this morbidity appears most clearly in the short story 'The Crime of Gabriel Gale'. The narrator of the story tells us that 'a very large number of young men nearly go mad', and that lots of boys 'are bursting with a secret and swelling morbidity'. He goes on to say that at that time there comes a dangerous moment:

> when the first connexion is made between the subjective and objective: the first real bridge between the brain and real things. It all depends on what it is; because, while it confirms his self-consciousness, it may happen to confirm his self deception.[3]

If, at this moment, the boy begins to think that every thing is within his own mind instead of outside it, he will believe that he can control it all, that he can be god in the sense of being a creator *ex nihilo*.
If one believes that one can control everything but finds that things are not totally obedient to one's control, then objects seem to

have a life of their own within one's mind while remaining separate from it. The self is divided against itself. The terror that results from the confusion of subjective and objective is similar to that of the narrator of Sartre's *Nausea*, who says 'Objects should not touch because they are not alive . . . they are useful, nothing more. But they touch me, it is unbearable.' Even Sartre's descriptions of the physical distortions he experiences are uncannily close to Chesterton's. The 'morbidity' of youth is specifically the fear of the insanity of a solipsist view of the world. And for Chesterton it is counteracted by the existence of an external reality which can only be fully acknowledged through a belief in God.

The critical work on Stevenson is especially interesting for its discovery of the same conclusions in Stevenson's early life, and for the examination of how he relates his belief in God to his style. Chesterton implies that Stevenson first reacts against the cynicism of Schopenhauer and Wilde by turning to a belief in God. To express this belief he returns stylistically to the toy theatres of his childhood. It is impossible not to compare this with Chesterton's own fascination with the toy theatre. His father introduced him to them when he was a child, and many early essays are devoted to their charms. Its positive value for Stevenson lay, according to Chesterton, in the clear, clean and bright figures with their distinct form and colour. He gave the function of the mind dramatic, active expression in precise gesture; he used compact, exact hieroglyphics. To other artists of the eighties and nineties the use of his precise figures was too much like a 'Moral Emblem'; but Stevenson needed this style because he had a specific message about the world, a belief in a specific God that demanded a definite form.

The use of these toy theatre figures also had a negative aspect, which Chesterton presents with sensitivity. The characters 'are aspects or attitudes of men rather than men'. They are two-dimensional and thin, without any ability to communicate real life, and indeed simplify its complexity. When he looks at the 'message' about God being expressed, he finds Stevenson stating the idea that God is power, and he adds, that power is God. The critic rejects the concept as far too simple a belief for such an intelligent man, and because of it, the 'message' is lacking when it comes. Finally Chesterton links Stevenson with William Morris as men who understood the need for responsible art but lacked the philosophy to make the art valuable.

In *Robert Louis Stevenson* we see Chesterton in the last decade of his career looking back to his formative years as man and writer. He demonstrates that God has to exist in order to counteract the morbidity and solipsism of the imagination, yet criticises an approach to God solely as a power as naive and insulting to the intelligence. But Chesterton realises that some approach is necessary. There is a definite need for God in a man who is anti-materialist because of the limited vision materialism can generate, yet also anti-pessimist and anti-impressionist because of the potential for the madness of solipsism that exists without an external authority. Similarly, while criticising Stevenson's use of emblems as over-simplifying the complexities of man, he can see the positive nature of the clarity, craftsmanship, and moral responsibility in his work. The emblem may be limited in use, but it points in the right direction of action and solid expression as opposed to impressionism.

Yet where was Chesterton in the nineties to find this necessary God, this clearer style? It is essential to remember that the search for and inquiry into the nature of God was not confined to religion. One discipline much concerned with the problem was sociology. During the eighties and nineties Herbert Spencer's *Principles of Sociology* was published; so was Frazer's *Golden Bough*, and much of Andrew Lang's work on myth and ritual in relation to society. The issue at stake seems to have been whether religion was initially only a propitiation of the gods, or whether it was an act of belief in them. In other words, was it a social convenience or a necessary and inevitable mystical belief? Chesterton's Unitarian background and general interests would have put him in contact with these writings. But also in 1894 he started work as a reader for a publishing house and gives some amusing accounts of the sociological theories he has to read through. [4] The following six years as a reader for Fisher Unwin would have inevitably exposed him to many of the current trends.

While the sociological theorists differ in their treatment of the central question, they all eventually point to agnosticism and science as the answer. In each case the propitiatory act is closely connected to formal religion. Even William James's *Varieties of Religious Experience*, written in 1904, which emphasised psychological rather than sociological aspects, makes the same distinction. In his view institutional religion is propitiatory and personal religion is true religion. James does, however, stress that belief is a more solid experience than agnosticism. Chesterton, coming from an agnostic background and surrounded by theories such as these, did not rush into formal religion. But, he needed a definite sense of an external

God. It is a safe conjecture that at the end of the 1890s he was very close to James's concept of personal religion.

One point emphasised and re-emphasised by all these men was the intrinsic relation between art and religion. The connection was important to the social theorists because their concept of religion made communication essential. But what is interesting is that all also note the unsatisfactory nature of the communication of the existence or propitiation of the God through art. A serious question results: If art is essentially tied to religious experience in that it relates that experience to man and society, how is it to do so effectively? The question is basically that which the older Chesterton asked Robert Stevenson when assessing the relationship between Stevenson's emblematic style and his idea of God, and asked of himself when he was a young man.

During the 1890s Chesterton assumed that he had only two artistic solutions: impressionism and rationalism. In 1927 Chesterton recalls the role Oscar Wilde played in his youth as the representative of the Impressionist movement. He was the nihilism, pessimism and decadence incarnate. It is probably true to say that this was the general opinion. The view certainly persisted, even appearing in the *Encyclopaedia Britannica* of 1911, and Chesterton's appraisal of Wilde in *The Victorian Age in Literature* (1913) gives only grudging credit to *De Profundis* and Wilde's conversion.

For Chesterton, Wilde was indissolubly linked with impressionism, and impressionism he later defined as sceptical and subjective, concerned with form and not with reality. In the parody of aestheticism in *Greybeards at Play* (1900) Chesterton presents the chaos to which this search for personal forms, if taken to its logical extreme, is reduced, and what concerned him then was the ease with which impressionism could become solipsism since in it objectivity is lost. Wilde himself is connected to these 'luxurious horrors of paganism' in the Decadent movement. But these attitudes are given in hindsight, at a time when the writer has achieved some critical distance. It should be noted that in the early 1890s he was caught up in the idea, and found it to have more apparent basis than 'thin and third-rate' materialism.

Chesterton's linking of Wilde with an overwhelming sense of the potential for solipsism is ironic when we consider that much of stylistic ground Wilde covered was later rediscovered by Chesterton. What would certainly have surprised Chesterton is Wilde's consciousness of the limitation of art. Rather than the impressionist telling someone that form was all as Chesterton had interpreted, Wilde would have said that the artist could never reproduce reality and therefore it was preferable to acknowledge the limitation by producing obviously fictive work. Chesterton's later distinction between truth and fiction pointed out that because the latter was man-made it was more congenial to the mind. This is a direct if unconscious echo of Wilde's declaration that exaggeration is necessary lest novels become 'so life-like that no one can possibly believe in their probability'. The need for exaggeration is rephrased elsewhere as a need for limits specifically to avoid 'impressionism' and 'rationalism'. Wilde also stresses the value of the concrete nature of an image. An idea is not valuable unless it interacts with an image:

> Truth in Art is the unity of a thing with itself: the outward rendered expressive of the inward: the soul made incarnate: the body instinct with spirit. [5]

Saint Francis is mentioned as being the first man to achieve this 'transsubstantiation' in which 'form reveals'. Chesterton will reflect all these facets of Wilde later in his career.

Where Wilde can appear obscure and where he undoubtedly annoyed Chesterton, is in his early idea of the 'improvement' of nature by art. There is a sense in which Wilde really means it; he genuinely preferred art to nature. However, its more profound meaning is that art finds forms and order for the potential chaos of nature and life; and as long as one realises that the forms are not nature itself, this is valuable. Of course, when a man's art becomes a perversion of, and substitute for, nature this is suspect.

What encourages the substituting of man's art for nature is Wilde's concept of the relation between religion and art, which is highly ambiguous. A consideration, especially of the Christian church, creeps into his work in De Profundis which was first and partially published in 1905. In it the separation between God and man is acknowledged, but the issue is confused by statements that all men have this dualism within them, and that Christ was able to realise it most intensely. It is Christ's ability to see the 'wonder' in things that Wilde takes as a type of his human, as opposed to his divine, characteristics. The ambiguity of these views leaves the creative power of man in question. Can he, by right of the divinity in himself, impose his forms on nature? Or is the divine external to him, and nature not under his governance? It was not unusual that Chesterton in the nineties considered Wilde an exponent of a theory which made man supremely divine and left the possibility of solipsism wide open. And it is not surprising that as Chesterton became aware of this danger he discarded what he thought was the style along with the philosophy.

Chesterton's alternative solution was rationalism or didactic art. Possibly the greatest influence on this stream of writing in the nineties was Tolstoy, although his *What is Art?* was not published in translation until 1898. Far more popular and persuasive, and not uninfluenced by Tolstoy, was Bernard Shaw. It was during the 1890s that his plays were first performed on London stages, and in 1898 the first collection of the plays with their prefaces appeared. We shall return to Shaw more fully later on; here it is only necessary to recognise the elements in the prefaces which would have both attracted and repelled Chesterton.

Most appealing would probably have been Shaw's belief in the total interdependence of art, life and religion. This would have made impossible both crimes of impressionism: the isolation of art from reality and the solipsistic vision. The interdependence of life, art and religion generates the moral quality of drama because it concerns the actions of a man's life. Shaw goes so far as to say that drama has to appeal didactically and to the intellect because the art of expressing feeling can only be performed by music.

Chesterton would have admired the plays for the sense of definite opinion which orders chaos. The preface to 'Widowers' Houses' baldly states that, 'It is a propagandist play – a didactic play – a play with a purpose'. But he might have more appreciated the honesty of this logical stylistic approach if it were based on a philosophy which he could share. Because Shaw writes from real life the didactic aspect of his plays is dependent on what he finds in life; and what he finds is contrary to any sense of 'wonder'. In one preface he defends his didactic approach solely on the grounds of his own negative vision:

> It is not my fault, reader, that my art is the expression of my sense of moral and intellectual perversity rather than my sense of beauty. My life has been passed mostly in big modern towns, where my sense of beauty has been starved whilst my intellect has been gorged with problems like that of the slums.[6]

Apart from the disagreement that Chesterton would have had with this 'materialist' vision of the world, Shaw, like Tolstoy, had a very relative view of philosophy and religion at this time. Similarly, the stress laid on opinion as the essential aspect of style is explained by the statement that the quality of a book is not in 'the opinions that is propagates, but the fact that the writer has opinions'. Stylistically, Shaw provides Chesterton with tools he has no need for; they express a different, materialist world. From the religious point of view he can also help little, his own interpretation and understanding being entirely relative.

The two streams of impressionist and rationalist art are widely divergent and Chesterton could belong to neither. He associated the aesthetic movement with instability and chaos. While Wilde was trying to find a way out in the pursuit of concrete imagery and allusive expression, the fundamental assumption that man cannot exactly describe what he sees overshadowed the value of these advances because of Chesterton's fear of solipsism. Although Chesterton eventually came to state this limitation of man himself, he was initially left with the idea of the artist as without definition and the man without order. On the other hand, those artists who appeared to be exponents of order had a stylistic approach which was coldly uncongenial, and a religious attitude too relative to provide stability. Chesterton was left anti-impressionist because of existential doubt and the fear of madness, and anti-rationalist because of his vision of 'wonder'. The same two elements in his make-up turned him almost necessarily towards a religion which was not agnostic, but personal and mystical. Yet when he wanted to express his religious belief, he could not verbalise it, since the available styles led back to impressionism and rationalism. Neither alternative offered a way out of the pessimism of the time, yet both had attractive elements. It is not surprising that Chesterton's journalistic and critical reaction to the period is confused and contradictory, or that his artistic efforts are primarily 'nonsense', acting as an antidote to cynicism.

2 Confused Trails: 1898—1903

Throughout his career Chesterton's artistic work was always the experimental ground for his criticism. The short stories, poems and novels always contained the seeds for future developments in the criticism. But the major works of criticism, with their conscious examination and expansion of the artistic ideas, seem to have been necessary to leave the way free for the artist to find new modes of expression. Chesterton's early artistic work (1891—1900), apart from his religious and political poetry, consists mainly of exercises in nonsense. Except for the purposes of parody, Chesterton rarely uses nonsense after 1900, and 'The Wild Knight', written in 1899, represents an attempt to find a new form for his serious literature.

In 1900 Chesterton took the plunge into self-employment, mainly in an effort to earn a salary adequate enough to enable him to marry his fiancée Frances Bloggs. He left the publishing house of Fisher Unwin on the strength of his journalistic work for *The Speaker* and 'The Daily News'. From 1900—4, he was preoccupied with making a career for himself as a journalist and critic, and the artistic work was put aside. But 'The Wild Knight' also contains serious formal obscurities that needed to be worked on and resolved. Many of the problems that it raises provide the matter for Chesterton's criticism of the intervening years; yet it is not until *Robert Browning*, his first major critical work, that they appear to have been even partially resolved.

Chesterton's criticism from 1898 to 1903, the year when he wrote *Robert Browning*, is a terrain criss-crossed with exploratory trails. But there is an overwhelmingly important concern motivating each excursion: the total relationship of man, mind and body, with life and with the inspiration of life which is God. An important essay which attempts to establish Chesterton's own attitude to art, life and finally God, is found in 'The Daily News' of 1902. 'Art and the Churches' concludes with the observation that former ages were correct in placing religion first, morality second, and art third:

All the schools of morality have as a fact come out of some
agreement about the government of things [religion], and all art
has come out of the exultation and excitement of that agreement. [1]

A month later Chesterton goes even further to the roots and states
that one's 'fundamental notion' of the world is a product of the
imagination. As long as one's

> imagination remains relentless and insatiable, so long it will
> produce religion, and morality and humanitarianism. Man, the
> moment he is man, must attempt to be the universe . . . [for] man
> alone among animals was an image of God. [2]

It is at this radical point that all the conflicts in Chesterton's early work
lie. Art is what separates man from the animals; it expresses his divine
function. Through it man aspires to be the image of God, yet he must
not blaspheme by trying to be God himself; this is the 'thought that
stops thought' and the root of solipsism.

In the early comments on religion Chesterton implies that God
communicates directly to man by giving him the power and the
imagination to perceive God in the world around him and this
'wonder' is the basis of his personal religion. Each man has a different
vision of life, and organised religion is of correspondingly little value.
However, the articles show him gradually shifting to a more formal
religious attitude. Slowly, the critic begins to study religion as a
limiting structure. In March 1903 Chesterton says that religion is a
positive way of pointing to 'the existence of a spiritual world'. He
then turns to it as something that embodies the irrational, and
continues to condemn its static dogma by saying that the 'Chaos is the
characteristic of the way that we all learn, and while we learn from it
we ought to remember that it is Chaos'. [3]

Barely seven months later, after a prolonged newspaper debate
with Blatchford of *The Clarion* on the nature of belief, Chesterton is
declaring himself a dogmatic Christian. On 19 December 1903 in a
column titled 'On Irrelevancy' Chesterton produces an early mani-
festo of his Christian belief. But it still reflects many of the conflicts of
his philosophy. He now uses the phrase 'mystical dogma' to express a
strong feeling for common sense. Yet there is a new strain. The writer
also believes that a human being called Christ stood to God 'in a
certain unique transcendental relationship which we call sonship'.
Life is seen to be logical and orderly only within these beliefs. These

statements themselves are only four months away from the extra-ordinary comment that, 'Impressionism is but Christianity to a canvas'. Chesterton is trying to bind together the conflicting desires for both personal vision and external order.

Chesterton's personal vision depends from the beginning on the perception of the uniqueness of objects. But despite his insistence on the importance of physical matter, he, at this stage, emphasises the greater importance of the essence. An interesting essay called 'Dreams' points to the 'absolute unity of emotion' experienced in dreams.[4] It goes on to attribute this unity to the feeling that while 'material circumstances' may alter, the essence of an act or an object is preserved so that 'existence betrays itself'. The essence experienced is the unity of the object's 'attitude to God'. Consequently the appearance of an object has little to do with its value. This is, of course, the argument used twenty-five years later to criticise the impressionists in *Autobiography*. It is not until he has written *Robert Browning* that Chesterton realises the danger of the mental outlook.

The division between appearance and essence has serious implications for Chesterton's conception of morality. Morality is considered to be the essence of man. It is the attitude to life generated by one's spiritual vision, of which one is mostly unaware. This idea of morality allows Chesterton to link the solidly material Velasquez with the impressionist Whistler. He says that 'in this wider sense of morality Velasquez is as much a moralist as Mr Whistler'. As late as 1903 the critic notes that 'Whistler the painter gave what the healthy moralist gives — hints'. Hand in hand with his praise of the 'L'art pour l'art' movement for their expression of spontaneous morality goes a condemnation of didactic morality. In 'A Re-Issue of Tolstoi' that author is deflated as 'a small and noisy moralist' in the strongly felt statement that:

> an artist teaches far more by his mere background and properties, his landscapes, his costume, his idiom and technique — all the part of the work, in short, of which he is probably entirely unconscious, than by the elaborate and pompous moral dicta he fondly imagines to be his opinions.[5]

Yet the view is in pointed conflict with Chesterton's concurrent beliefs that morality is to be praised for being something definite. Critics who condemn paintings for being 'moral', implying that they have specific meaning, are severely chastised in 'Literary Pictures of the Year', and we must not forget that central essay 'Art and the Churches'. Morality is an 'agreement about the government of all things'; and modern life is to be pitied for failing to realise the agreement into 'a new philosophy of existence'.

It is not surprising that many of the comments on morality coincide with those on art. Art is seen as an expression of that morality, that essence of man. Chesterton's article on Tolstoy refines the concept by postulating a direct connection between the vision of life at that time still with the emphasis on personal religion and ethics, and art. He says that good art will present the essence of man in the work itself, while bad art will present the essence as something specifically told to us. It is on the basis that good art expresses morality within itself, that Chesterton claims art to be 'far more moral than anything else'. He also notes that since the essence of man is his vision of life, good art, expressing this essence, can never be separated from life.

Just as it has been emphasised that morality is more valuable if unconscious, so too is art. Poetry is described as 'an animal thing, and the more spiritual for that'. The dislike for the conscious, the didactic and the philosophical is the foundation for Chesterton's criticism of Tolstoy; and Schopenhauer and Carlyle are both specifically praised only for the moments when they are more artist than philosopher. A hair's breadth away from this picture of the unconscious artist is the decadent artist. He might seem to fulfil the conditions of a 'good' artist for he employs no rigid lines in his expression; he swerves away from didactic forms. Yet Chesterton at this stage says that to be an 'artist in life' one must be mad; one becomes a 'horrible fairy-tale of a man constantly changing into other men'. It appears that the artist must walk a tight-rope between the conflicting tensions of control and spontaneity.

The conflict arises from the same source as the conflict in Chesterton's religious and moral attitudes. Broadly speaking, he is judging literature according to whether or not it expresses a God-inspired essence. The impressionists, or aesthetes and decadents appear to express no essence whatsoever, and the rationalists and didactics tend towards a man-made essence that stifles the God-inspired. Good art, in expressing a God-inspired essence, expresses a vision of life or a religion; and Chesterton acknowledges the vital connection between religion and art. Art can express the limits with which religion counteracts madness. While Chesterton accepts that man wants to create because he is made in the image of God, he also sees that both

impressionist and rationalist attempt to become God. They attempt
to escape from the limitations of man by imposing their own ideas as
the sole criteria.

Man is caught in what the author discusses under the title 'The
Conundrum of Art'. When an artist expresses something, he usually
finds himself having to say what that thing is. In doing so he is
bounded not only by his personal perception, but also by the very
connotation of the words he uses. The conundrum of art is that 'to
define a thing is literally and grammatically to limit it, and this is to
limit the illimitable'. If an artist attempts to make his own definition
the only acceptable one, he is assuming that he can create with the
same perfection as God. He is limited by the fact that he cannot see his
own limitations. However, in avoiding the limits of definition the
artist may come perilously close to expressing nothing at all, for artists
may concentrate on the destruction of any definition rather than the
suggestion of one. Both impressionist and rationalist create assuming
that their art is justified in itself and that that art alone is absolute
because it alone is not connected with the vagueness of the external
world; and both deny the role of ultimate authority to God. Working
from this conclusion Chesterton increasingly realises that formal
religion may provide a resolution to the conflicts within both his
vision of life and his moral ideas. Concurrently he comes to assess
literature not merely on its sense of God-inspired essence, but further
on its expression of this essence within a form externally guided by
religious belief.

The form of art itself receives more attention as Chesterton
attempts to resolve the conflicts within his philosophy. As he does so,
he gradually becomes aware of the danger of over-emphasising the
importance of essence. In any type of art the absence of insistence on
form in the style may lead to a separation of the essence from life and
its inspiration. It becomes apparent that certain styles will be more
conducive to expressing essence correctly than others. A further
corollary is that artistic failure may come to indicate moral failure;
good art is not only morally good but stylistically good. At this time
Chesterton has certainly not yet organised his criticism quite so far,
but a statement in the Bookman Booklet of 1903, *Charles Dickens*,
points in this direction. Dickens is heavily criticised for a 'comfortable' optimism that makes him play at being a despot with his
characters. He will give a happy ending when a more profound
optimism would allow the characters their own existence and their
own tragedies.

What Chesterton is exploring in these early years is the danger of personal distortion inherent in different techniques. But underlying this is a fear that expression may not be possible at all. In a letter to his future wife Frances on the death of her sister he says that 'for real peace, no human words are much good except perhaps some of the unfathomable, unintelligible, unconquerable epigrams of the Bible'; and after trying to comfort her anyway, asks forgiveness for 'the verbosity of one whose trade it is to express the inexpressible'.

The first real awareness that Chesterton has of technical failure derives from his study of impressionism. That the author initially had a greater fear of a narrowing rationalistic form than impressionism is indicated by his praise for impressionists such as Whistler. Yet the critic of 'Literary Pictures of the Year' imputes a boredom to 'that Impressionist twilight'. His attack on the decadents points out that 'the end of all this impressionism is that maddening horror of unreality'. A later article notes not 'incompleteness, but a shading and fading away'. In this case 'incompleteness' would suggest potential completion, definition. Chesterton's point is that the intent of impressionism is purposely to leave things vague and undefined.

All other artistic techniques contain the potential for the failure of expression so often met with in impressionism. Symbolism at its best is a form of mysticism. Shakespeare is described as a symbolist because:

> he represents the mysterious mental connection between shapes and ideas which must finally defeat any purely technical view . . . [6]

This type of style is one that becomes important to Chesterton when he recognises the need for fusing essence with appearance. It even becomes synonymous in his vocabulary for 'poetry'. However it is limited by its ever-present potential for becoming purely associative, random and arbitrary. It is also a very personal technique that may become hinderingly obscure. A technique less open to failure in communication although correspondingly more limited in potential, is heraldry or emblem. An early article notes the advantage of emblems which suggest not define, and communicate through the heart not the intellect. Yet emblem itself may limit communication of an event to an image that is too specific. The specific nature of an image can leave it inadequate because it severs too many connections with the external actuality of the event. The result is that it remains important only in what it can convey by itself and does not call upon real experience of the event.

The only other technique Chesterton mentions in his criticism, and that very briefly, is allegory. He makes an interesting point that 'portraits are allegories for the simple reason that all men are allegories, puzzles, earthly stories with heavenly meanings . . .'. But the definition exists side by side with the observation that medieval dream allegories are devoid of any essential truth because they are obviously didactic and abstract in interest. Yet it is interesting that an early letter discusses allegory as almost an unartistic mode of expression. He speaks of making his future home 'symbolic. Not artistic' and goes on to ridicule the aesthetes. What he wants 'is to make a house really allegoric: really explain its own essential meaning'. But this line of inquiry is, for the moment, unpursued.

Quite probably Chesterton's increasing awareness of form is responsible for his growing dislike and eventual hatred of impressionism. Yet it should be emphasised that if there is a shift of opinion it is very slight. The nature of a newspaper column necessitates a daily assessment of one's ideas; this will naturally yield vacillating and contrary opinions in a young mind exploring new terrain. Only a distanced overview can detect change; and if anything, what the reader finds is more of a shift in emphasis in the conflicts rather than a change. The roots of the author's acceptance of form can be found in a column written as early as 1901 called 'Browning and his Ideal'. Here he says that it is

> one of the curses of the criticism of poetry that it tends to detach the ideas of a poet from the forms by which he expresses them. . . .[7]

Not surprisingly, it is in *Robert Browning*, the major critical work of 1903, that Chesterton attempts to resolve the artistic and therefore the moral and religious conflicts of his world.

ii

Chesterton's theme in *Robert Browning* arises from his disagreement with the accepted opinion that Browning was primarily concerned with the ideas and not with the form of his art. He believes that the prevailing misinterpretation of Browning's poetry was due to a misunderstanding of the poetic form. Early readers of Browning did not realise that apparent carelessness and obscurity in the work was a function of the meaning rather than a disregard for style. As a result they had, on the one hand, emphasised the intellectual meaning despite the form, and on the other, neglected any meaning that form might contain. Chesterton tells the contemporary reader to observe and try to understand the interaction between the form and the meaning. He suggests that the techniques of style will reflect the process of the function of the imagination. The imagination itself will directly present the vision of life that the poet holds. The reader will then perceive the soul rather than the mind of the man; he will be close to understanding the unconscious urges of the life, that are so much more valuable than the intellectual arguments that may be pursued.

Central to the critical interpretation of this book is Chesterton's discussion of the two main types of poet. The first is the poet speaking about a situation, which comes close to the rationalistic and didactic aspect of art. The second is the poet speaking from within a situation, a generation of immediate experience that can devolve into impressionism. A stanza of a poem by Goldsmith is used to describe the didactic function of the poet as the *vates*. Goldsmith gives

> his own personal and definite decision upon it, entirely based upon general principles, and entirely from the outside. (170)

In contrast, two comparable stanzas from a poem by Burns express the 'song of experience'. There is no personal judgement within the poem; and the experience is completely beyond definition by general principles. When the critic comes to Robert Browning's poetry he describes it in terms of a tension between the two. Browning attempts to find a truth beyond the purely didactic approach of personal rationalism, a truth made up of individual emotional experience within a situation. Yet he also attempts to be just and impartial to the experience as a whole, to a situation with its own intrinsic value.

The tension that Chesterton suggests is one between control and spontaneity. The poet who wishes to go further than the didactic denies himself absolute moral control. Yet Browning's aim at a 'truth' implies a final morality beyond the individual. From another point of view the decision to search for truth in spontaneous emotional responses may result in finding no stable moral. Yet to begin with a stable moral implies an unnatural limitation. It becomes apparent that Chesterton wants the reader to look to the inter-relationship of form and meaning for a resolution to this tension.

Despite the fact that Browning is constantly described as 'unconscious', 'natural', 'spontaneous' and 'impulsive', it is increasingly
emphasised that the important balancing counterweight is the poet's
consciousness of form which provides a necessary moral control.

The examination of the tension begins with the poet's imagination.
Browning perceives the importance of material detail in experience;
but he notes that this may lead to a total anarchy of the individual
objects considered. The loss of control by an author over a detail or an
individual event allows it to become important only in itself rather
than in its contribution to the whole work. This isolation of detail
often reduces it to a number or a sign in a manner similar to the loss of
potency of an image when it is withdrawn from the symbolic
complex that generated it. It retains rational meaning only in itself
and if transposed into another symbolic complex will appear
irrational because it is not relating to the whole. In this way the detail
degenerates into the impressionism of emblems with arbitrary
meanings unrelated to the total experience. But Browning is also
aware of the concrete reality of the total experience. The detail is
constantly forced to function not as an emblem for an abstract idea to
be intellectually appreciated, but as a metaphor which contains the
meaning of the idea and causes an emotional response. The poet does
not believe that 'a flower is symbolical of life', but that 'life, a mere
abstraction, is symbolical of a flower'. His perception that the
communication of experience demands the inclusion of feeling rather
than intellect allows him to generate emotional value and an
apprehension of the personal truth in a situation.

Chesterton assumes that it is in order to emphasise the detail within
experience that Browning develops the technique of the grotesque.
The grotesque creates a new perspective on detail that wakes the
observer up to its potential. The grotesque means 'energy, the
energy which takes its own way'. Chesterton observes that many
aspects of the grotesque are similar to nonsense; and nonsense is a
technique that he understands well from his own artistic work. The
effect of nonsense, and of the grotesque, is to remove the rational and
the connotations habitually made about a situation. What remains is
the essential force and value of that event, and this is the point at
which nonsense makes its exit. The grotesque however builds back
into a type of caricature. It gives back to the situation the parts of its
external being that are directly related to the essence that has been
uncovered. In a similar way as the cartoonist who will emphasise a
facial feature, or a satirist who may draw attention to a verbal

mannerism, the grotesque gives shape to the fundamentals of the situation experienced. The detail is released from its unimportant surroundings into a curtailed and grotesque form that emphasises yet controls its meaning.

The use of the grotesque is partly responsible for a superficial obscurity in Browning that Chesterton discusses at the beginning of the book. The creation of new perspectives which are obvious to the author may also be too personal to be understood by an external observer. Of course, when one does come to understand the perspective, its new vision will be all the more powerful for having been previously hidden. But obscurity as a technique in itself also appears in Browning's poetry. Chesterton suggests that this obscurity is not due to the discussion of obscure subjects as in the work of Meredith; hence it must have more of a stylistic character. Browning's obscurity is interpreted as an attempt to suggest the full value of an experience by consciously generating an impression of incompleteness, since it lies beyond his ability to express meaning fully. The critic implies that the experience of all the details within the poem seem to add up to more than the situation can account for. He concludes that life cannot be totally explained and we are foolish to ask for such an explanation.

A third and most important technique derives from the sense of the whole being greater than the sum of its parts. To examine this aspect, Chesterton turns to *The Ring and the Book*. The poem contains the by now familiar tension. It is 'representative of all modern development' away from didactic external control; yet it contains an internally generated control. It is the method rather than the intellectual idea of the book that directs one to the 'centre of spiritual guilt and the corresponding centre of spiritual rectitude'. In the same way that Browning acknowledges the importance of detail, so too he acknowledges the importance of the individual point of view; and each point of view is considered to be morally valid. The problem here is that the poet may end up with a moral anarchy on his hands. Furthermore, the same material facts being presented in such shifting perspectives may leave the experience totally unrecognisable and impressionistic. The resolution is found in the stylistic method that creates parts giving value to individual perspective, but never allowing it absolute truth. The absolute truth is only discovered when the poem has been finished; when the multiplicity of perspectives comes under an overruling moral guidance. The partial truths accumulate into the whole experience, and the poet 'makes it ultimately appear that Pompilia was really right'.

Chesterton's critique has so far examined the tension between Browning's artistic expression of spontaneity and control, and concludes that in each case the detail and the whole must contribute to the meaning. The question now arises of what the moral overview implicit in the control achieves. The answer lies in a comparison of Browning with the impressionist poets. Both he and they are agreed in the essential importance of the individual point of view; both accept the elusiveness of truth and the intangibility of justice. The difference is that Browning concedes a partial knowledge of an eternal to the individual, rather than no knowledge at all. He believes in the existence of a final truth and in an absolute, yet mysterious, justice. Chesterton acknowledges that:

> It is really difficult to decide when we come to the extreme edge of veracity, when and when not it is permissable to create an illusion. (194)

Yet he personally believes that that decision has consciously to be made, and he congratulates the poet on making it.

Chesterton also acknowledges that once the decision is made 'no one surely need be ashamed to admit that such a rule is not entirely easy to draw up'. Here again he congratulates the poet on having found an acceptable non-didactic form for moral control. Browning's mysticism is once more the major point in his favour for:

> the great concrete experiences which God made always come first; his own deductions and speculations about them always second. (183)

This mysticism implies a vision of life in which the man, Browning, always realises the impossibility for him to understand himself intellectually, let alone the rest of the world. The techniques Chesterton has examined present the vision. Browning allows each man to speak for himself; but no individual is allowed to be the whole situation. Even the situation itself cannot contain the significance of its parts. In the first place we recognise the existence of some further potential which is complete. Both techniques demonstrate that while Browning guides and suggests he does not dictate. The ultimate humility is in the fact that the form reveals the poet's own incompleteness and imperfection; it is an acknowledgement of his own limitation that he only points to a fulfilment. What the view achieves is the ability to make decisions, yet let the decisions be God-inspired, not personal.

Having established that Browning failed neither on the side of the impressionists nor on that of didacticism, we must be aware of another aspect of him. Throughout the book Chesterton has carefully pointed out that Browning did not succeed by chance but by design. As an artist he opts ultimately for control. So the critic praises the poet for trying to include the spontaneous, emotional truth; and he also acclaims him for having succeeded in finding his own form of moral control. Browning's awareness of the incompleteness of man makes him quite conscious of the danger in didacticism. If a man is not perfect, his attempts at despotism will always contain some measure of fault and potential corruption. Chesterton interprets Browning's 'Strafford' as an examination of despotism, and notes that the despot progresses naturally to a 'blasphemous and lying assumption of Godhead'. If a political despot may so develop, so may an artistic despot. Browning is shown to be aware of the potential danger and to be consciously trying to avoid it.

Similarly Browning is conscious of the dangers of impressionism. His belief in the importance of individual details makes him strongly aware of the violent energy to be found in them. The poet realises that to give a heightened value to detail is but a step away from a 'desire to add a touch to things in the spirit of man', which is found in the poem 'Prince Hohensteil-Schwangau'. Since man is not perfect, his attempts at perfection will necessarily include some touch of madness. The belief that man is able to complete himself produces 'maniacs, isolated in separate cells'. The artist draws away from, and consciously controls, the potential insanity of this position. For Browning there is an unavoidable belief in a reality which is the existence of God and the corresponding incompleteness of man.

Browning's consciousness of God underlies his conscious morality and conscious form. In it Chesterton perceives the poet's unique resolution to the paradox that while man must strive after the divine to fulfil his humanity, he must never attempt to be divine. Throughout the book, but especially during the study of Browning's philosophy, statements have been made concerning the fact that poetry is the best means of communication of the act of creation. Since the vision of life is a perception of God's order, and since it is communicated best through poetry which reaches into the unconscious, any attempt to recreate God's plan, to imitate the divine, finds its medium in poetry. Chesterton says that the poet's greatest contribution is the recognition of this need in all men to be divine.

When the poet gives men the words necessary for communication, he also determines the form that communication will take. The moral judgement involved in this decision reveals the vision of the poet himself. Consequently Browning's characters directly imitate the poet's own relation to the problem of striving to be divine. Chesterton finds that each character has a 'definite and peculiar confidence of God', which Browning gives them the power to express. To communicate their belief they are given brief moments of poetry in which Browning demands, as in his personal poems, a moral direction which is an admittance of God. It is in this paradox that Chesterton sees the resolution of his major conflict: For Browning, the attempt to be divine through creation cannot be successful without the recognition of a divinity greater than oneself. The critic concludes his book by saying that the poet's characters, as well as the poet, both speak at times in a voice which is 'the voice of God, uttering His everlasting soliloquy'.

Robert Browning is Chesterton's first major critical effort. In it he attempts to apply and reconcile the exploratory statements of his journalistic criticism. He found in Browning an example of his own conflicts. On an artistic level the tension between the didactic and the impressionist holds sway in Browning's work. An appreciation of the poet's achievement of resolution in a definite, but not rigidly formal, control over spontaneous experience reflects Chesterton's slight shift towards form. The moral conflict which the artistic tension parallels is that between dogma and unconscious inspiration. Here the critic's emphasis on the consciousness of the poet in his application of formal moral control indicates another shift towards a sense of necessary consciousness in morality. On the most profound level, that of religion and the vision of life it expresses, Chesterton finds in Browning his own conflict between the necessity of attempting to express the divine and the blasphemy of believing that one can achieve it. The poet resolves the tension by demanding that the creator exist within the creation for any poetic fulfilment. This necessary absolute in art once more reflects an apparent tendency in Chesterton's early criticism. The shift of emphasis in the critical conflicts that was vaguely discerned is confirmed; and tentative resolutions have been reached from which new directions can be taken.

3 Artistic Explorations: 1892–1900

Chesterton's first major attempt at serious poetry was 'The Wild Knight', written in 1899. As a work of art it had many stylistic problems, and the poet was heavily criticised for obscurity. But it represents an effort to break away from the dominating forms of his early poetry and short stories. The incomprehension of the contemporary readers was largely a direct result of the poet's experimentation with a new form that was only partially successful. Not surprisingly, the form was a combination of the techniques of emblem and metaphor that were the subject of his early critical discussion on style.

Most of the early artistic efforts that have been published indicated a close intertwining between the artist's vision of life and a search for a specific technical means of communicating it. As one would expect from a man who quickly developed a perceptive critical faculty, much of the art represents a series of studies in the conventions of communication. In order to examine literary styles a large number of poems and short stories employ a personally adapted form of the techniques of nonsense literature. But there is a separate stream of purely religious poetry which is quite different in purpose. Significantly, the earliest examples of Chesterton's art that are available belong to this group of poems. On the whole they are not concerned with modes of expression but with the vision of life itself. They are far closer to the original impulses and essence of man, and the very early work disparages the whole concept of art as a satisfactory form of human communication.

Within Chesterton's religious poetry there is a definite division in tone. The earlier works are primarily negative, both in content and style, while much of the later poetry is positive, concentrating on the 'wonder' of the world. A poem of 1891, 'Adveniat Regnum Tuum',[1] is a good example of the earlier kind. There is an overwhelming negativity about the poem in its ignoring of free-will and human responsibility. And the negativity is reflected in the juxtapositions of words which empty each other of meaning and in the drawn out repetitiveness and similarity of the couplets. What is surprising in the poem of doubt is the running energy of youth. If man has no power, the poet is going to insist on despair with the heavy-handed grasp of a fatalistic cement driller.

Of course the poet is here a boy not yet seventeen years old. One should expect neither technical virtuosity nor philosophical maturity. What is interesting is the consistency of the negative approach, the reluctance to describe the greatness that lies beyond his powers and the corresponding emphasis on human weakness. As the poet matures, the negative approach acquires interesting tension. Gradually, the negative aspects of religion are related to the church and ironically this begins to indicate the positive aspects of religion in the existence of God and his direct inspiration of man.

The division between formal religion and inspiration remains as important an idea in Chesterton's early artistic work, as it became in the criticism. Most of the elusive quality connected with inspiration is transformed into the positive process of Chesterton's 'wonder' poems. But one poem, 'The Song of Labour' written in 1892,[2] can be viewed as transitional, and relates the division to different kinds of expression. The poem is interesting because in it the negativity is juxtaposed with man's attempt to manifest inspiration. There is an important distinction between formal religion and politics which 'rest upon words' and the 'voice' of the labourers which can communicate directly. The poem concludes by saying that art too is inadequate in providing an expression of nature; only the labourer in his pure actions can hear 'The roar of the endless purpose'.

It is apparent that throughout these early poems Chesterton is ideologically opposed to form of any kind because it is potentially limiting. The belief is generated by a spiritual division between inspiration and formal religion; and a human division between action which is direct and art which proceeds through a form. The apparent dismissal of art as a means of expressing inspiration is obviously undermined by the very fact that Chesterton has chosen to write poetry, not to mention the extreme formality of its presentation. It is possibly the implied frustration of his attempts to express himself adequately that makes the poems so negative. The positive process of the 'wonder' poems, on the other hand, is quite simply a celebration of the incomprehensibility of the world rather than a lament for man's limited understanding. Technically it freely admits and manipulates rather than regrets man's inadequate expression. The process also depends upon a sense of free-will, and an overwhelming belief in the beneficent presence of a God.

An early poem which is religious in its discussion of man's vision of life is 'By the Babe Unborn' from 1892.[3] The techniques used are almost the opposite to the negative poems. Rather than using similarity and repetition to create a sense of waiting, the poet attempts to make the vision of the poem quite different from anything we would expect. Instead of talking about form he manipulates it so that it appears to shift and change. Rather than presenting a juxtaposition of dogma and inspiration, the poet creates in us the experience of inspiration that transcends dogma in its personal relevance. The poem attempts to refresh one's perspective and make one recognise the wonder of a world infused with God's power. Further developments of the positive poetry in the later poems of the 1890s such as 'The Holy of Holies' or 'The Earth's Shame' show Chesterton experimenting with paradox and ambiguity as means of indicating the presence of God.

The two processes of expression in the religious poems show a rooted division in both thought and style. The negative process describes the weakness of man and the inadequacy of formalised responses used by the priest or artist. When it attempts to postulate a resolution in the ways of God working through man, it invariably results in contradiction. The 'wonder' poems, on the other hand, indicate the amazing vision man may have despite his limitations, if he stays close to intuitive inspiration which is God. Their celebration of God's worldly presence is normally expressed in paradox or mystery that admits inadequacy but resolves contradiction by emphasising the transcendent power of God. Both styles also find expression in the nonsense literature of the short stories and of a few poems. In the use of nonsense Chesterton goes further than a discussion of the vision of life itself to a study of the modes of communication for expressing the vision. Before examining the short stories, it is important to sort out the various techniques and meanings of nonsense literature and to understand why it should provide a suitable medium for Chesterton's thought at this time.

The purpose of nonsense is first of all to disrupt the process of normal order, and second, to impose an order which is usually rational on a vision of life that then seems chaotic. The two processes occur simultaneously since the nonsense rules are what make the ordinary rules appear chaotic. The ludicrous results are formed in the way the chaotic vision differs from normal experience. Yet the reader is also able to perceive the essential reality on which both logics stand. The tension produced is in the constant attempts to bring the actual world within the limitations of the nonsense inventor. While the nonsense writer tries to make a world out of the pattern of his own mind, he is constantly aware of the fact that he is doing so. The consciousness of the process forbids him to ever reach completion, because it would be at that point that the limitations of his mind would collapse under the force of actuality. Consequently a great part of nonsense concentrates on the rational details of life, the whole of which, as Emile Cammaerts points out, is never greater than the sum of its parts.[4]

The disintegration of normal life proceeds mainly by separating it into parts than can then be shown to have no rational relation to each other. Many nonsense writers make up words that are similar enough in sound and appearance for us to accept them as normal, so that the recognition of their difference upsets the perspective of actual life. Elizabeth Sewell suggests in her study of nonsense,[5] that there are few verbs present in nonsense literature because verbs indicate relationships between things. Her book also notes that many nonsense books are illustrated, and suggests that the use of pictures restricts an image to a specific interpretation, so that the usual associations cannot be made. The need for objective control on the part of the inventor also results in the use of few emotive words, because they have personal connotations that cannot be controlled. But each of these methods implies a logic on the part of the author. The invention of new words and the drawing of pictures contain within themselves the order of the writer's mind. The only way to have normal vision make sense is to participate in the new kind of logic which is being used. There is no persuasion involved in the process. If the reader does not perceive the logic of the writer he will be able neither to accept its standards nor to believe that it has reduced the normal world to chaos. The purpose of nonsense is to offer the reader a logic which he can use to participate in the personal creation of another order. The more successfully he uses the logic the more able he is to control the events. The better the events are controlled the more obvious becomes the discrepancy between normal and invented logic, and the clearer the fundamental reality they share.

Within nonsense there are different attitudes to life. The person who invents nonsense is playing at being God as he creates his order. The purpose of the style depends on how he does so. He may want to convince us of his complete control or he may want to indicate his limitations and the inadequacy of his logic. Nonsense can simply be a game. The object here is to keep within the personal rules invented, to assume complete control of them within their personal limits. The control of objects becomes a fight with normality for the dominance of life. The purpose may have the function of a parody where a situation of normal life is shown to exist by conventional rules that easily become nonsense and put up little resistance. It may also consist of testing one's ability to control. This kind of nonsense writer tries to forget that these are human rules that he is inventing. He puts the full force of his intellect into proving that he can control everything. It is when the writer actually believes that he is God that nonsense comes close to the effect of fantasy.

It is worth pointing out now how fantasy differs from nonsense. The fantasist also generates a world of his own, but it comes out of the actual world rather than being an opposing one. Fantasists can therefore function normally within the relationships of life. The major difference between fantasy and nonsense is that fantasy tries to become unconscious of the limitations of its vision. To succeed, it depends upon the creation of a whole so complete that actuality does not intrude. The reader, far from actively participating, has everything done for him. He passively accepts the point of view he is being persuaded of. Interestingly enough, few active verbs are used in fantasy because relationships between things are being constantly explained by the author. The new worlds and even languages he invents are understood in the context of the fantastic world, rather than reality, and do not conflict with reality. The control is not exercised over the content itself, so much as over the reader's reactions to it. Consequently, one does not see how the logic works, but merely knows that it does. The existence of the persuasive force makes possible the misuse of propaganda. The fantasist who believes that his vision is the correct one also needs to persuade others of it. It is a power game in which only one person can play; everyone else is just an instrument for his manipulation. Both fantasist and nonsense-writer become insane when they genuinely forget that their created worlds are separate from actuality.

While the former purpose of nonsense was to convince the reader of the author's complete control over the logic, the second purpose is to indicate his limitations by exposing the inadequacy of his logic. This second form generally yields a more serious approach. Since the logic invented always tears away the normal standards, a situation could, as in some parodies, be shown to be totally based on convention with no intrinsic or organic rules that resists all the attacks by nonsense logic. However, when the logical reduction of a situation leaves a fundamental basis which is unalterable and cannot be effaced, the nonsense has performed the function of pointing out the root value of that situation. What resists nonsense lies beyond rational logic in the realm of reason. In this way nonsense operates as a form of paradox. It destroys normal relationships with its logical control in an attempt to uncover what is not controllable and therefore inde-structible; it manipulates rational logic to show what lies beyond that logic. This is probably what lies behind Elizabeth Sewell's statement that the nonsense of Edward Lear accepts God. If a nonsense writer is always making one aware of the ultimate limits of his logic, he is also by implication aware of an existence outside of his own. Rather than being an intellectual attack, Lear's nonsense is childlike. Its vagaries do not aim at creating a new world to destroy the standards of the existing one, but to test them. His nonsense is always humble, acknowledging his weakness; and it can never approach the insane, for it never tries to be God.

Although Chesterton uses nonsense in both main ways, he tends on the whole to use the more serious purpose. Remembering the important essay 'Dreams' and the distinction Chesterton makes between appearance and essence, it is understandable why nonsense is such an appropriate form. The essay discusses the fact that in dreams details tend to take over; they become too important. Consequently, art appears to be in opposition to dreams because art imposes a control over detail. Chesterton goes on to say that art's attempt to control the chaos of dreams is an incorrect understanding of what they generate. He points out that this chaos is necessary, that Biblical dreams are really great spiritual truths covered by 'farcical mysteries' and 'grotesque parables', seemingly without meaning. The dreams need an interpreter to get at their essence which lies behind the detail, but that the unordered detail is necessary to show that the external form is not important. The author then claims that great art alone correctly uses the technique of dreams by portraying a chaotic exterior to a genuine meaning. Both great art and dreams have an abiding unity of feeling directly related to the inspiration of God. The unity is the essence that lies beyond form. Nonsense can perform the function of reducing a situation to its basic inspiration, which in some cases does not exist. It is therefore technically highly suitable for a man who wishes to uncover the essential force behind a situation.

The negative process of Chesterton's religious poems can also be seen in the use of nonsense as parody. Here a method of logic is examined and applied according to the writer's own rules to test how far it fulfils what it says it can fulfil. Chesterton's examination of modes of communication by nonsense is normally concentrated on forms of art, such as 'A Fragment' of 1896, and the impossibility to present exactly what they claim to represent. But in the entertaining sketch 'Half-Hours in Hades', written in 1892,[6] Chesterton looks at the scientific method. The technique is based on the idea that a definition of a thing will help to understand and explain it. In this piece the narrator attempts to codify existing demons. The three sections examine definition, evolution and practical application of the basic information. Definition consists of the well-tested technique of taking words to their literal extreme. It is the main factor of Chesterton's nonsense logic. He plays around with the common or 'garden' serpent and the 'blue' devil. Both are illustrated according to a literal interpretation of the words describing their appearance.

The second section, on evolution, illustrates well Cammaerts's statement that parody is to literature what caricature is to art. Chesterton draws a series of simple figures side by side with a caricature of each of them that picks out the visual distinctions, and gives them another meaning by subjecting them to an odd artistic logic. For example, a man with handlebar moustaches and sabre-sword, becomes a devil with horns and tail.

By the third section the logic of the writer has been learnt by the reader. He can appreciate the parody by applying the rules himself. Consequently, when we discover that the final example is a witch, we understand Chesterton's point. When reduced to its ultimate degree of definition the scientific method cannot explain why the thing exists. The irony that results from this attempt at a definitive demonology is that the essential evil of them escapes. It cannot be defined or controlled.

The positive process of the 'wonder' poems also finds a counterpart in the serious nonsense that takes one to the startling discovery of essence that lies behind artistic structure. In 'The Wild Goose Chase' of 1892[7] Chesterton makes a study of the use of metaphor. In his early religious poems the author admires the man of action far more than the artist because the inspiration of life is directly communicated. Here the author again uses his nonsensical process of reducing a poetic form to its literal interpretation; and the boy of the story acts out the literal meaning of metaphorical images. The first event spells out the method and then the reader is left on his own. When one recognises the verbal basis for the actions, he becomes aware of the meaning of the words. The process is made explicit in the final section when the boy, now a young man, realises that he has lost his youth in his quest for the wild goose. His whole life has been a 'wild goose chase' that only ends with his death. The nonsense illuminates the essential origin of words by stripping them of their conventional use and exposing their real human value.

The participation in the logic of positive nonsense removes conventional meanings and leaves the essence. The process also demonstrates the serious reservations that the young Chesterton has about form because it can be so misleading. All Chesterton's forms of nonsense essentially agree with the conclusion of the negative religious poems: that art, because of its form is incapable of expressing essential meaning. Although nonsense was entirely appropriate to his needs at that time, it sidetracked him from the valuable experiments with mystery and paradox in the positive religious poems. His nonsense, by its very method of demolishing artistic structures, defeats the aim of poetry or art by denying that they can communicate. Because the artist is handicapped by form, Chesterton chose to destroy it by showing its meaninglessness. Yet this is similar to the paradoxical denial of, yet use of form in the religious poems. Nonsense could not expose essence without form existing first as a vehicle for communication. More importantly, it is nonsense as a form itself that Chesterton had to manipulate very carefully, just because he did not want it to interfere with essential meaning. In this we see the paradox of the nonsense technique. It did not take him long to realise his position, and appreciate consciously what he had unconsciously been doing.

The concept of a necessary vehicle for communication and the care with which he had to control his nonsense led Chesterton to recognise that some forms could be more appropriate than others to express essence. While the examination of metaphors and words in his short stories led to a destruction of their conventional, over-used and often carelessly accepted meaning, it also led to a rediscovery of their original value as images for experience. The problem remains that the poet cannot demonstrate the value of words every time he uses them, so they lie constantly in danger of becoming conventional again. One sees Chesterton realising that the techniques of expression come to define the relationship between the body of words and the essence. As a result the form begins to contribute to the communication rather than merely being a vehicle. Since some techniques will be more appropriate to convey some essences, the artist has a conscious duty to choose a form.

As this awareness grows, Chesterton not only becomes willing to value words and colours, but also begins to discard the nonsense form. The process of stripping off the outside appearance of an object in order to see its essence becomes contradictory when form expresses essence. It is significant that Chesterton rarely uses nonsense for any purpose other than parody during the rest of his career. The first book that he published, *Greybeards at Play* (1900), contains only one serious nonsense poem: 'A Dedication'. At least the first four stanzas of this poem had been written and illustrated as early as 1893. The remaining three poems are parodies on pantheism, altruism and aestheticism respectively and use many of his well-tried nonsense techniques.

While Chesterton continues to use nonsense in order to parody, his more serious short stories take on another form. The new approach is fundamentally different from nonsense and closer to the developments in his positive religious poetry. Rather than destroying the potential logic in words or situations to reach the essence behind them, he explores the logic of expression to assess its relationship to essence. He is trying to find the best technique for expressing experience.

In 1897 Chesterton wrote a piece for the Slade School magazine *Quarto*. The story, 'A Crazy Tale', is a literal examination of the way words assume value. The main character is one of those 'tall spare' men who populate the non-rational sides of Chesterton's literature. He proceeds to describe an incredible experience, whose meaning he has forgotten, to someone he meets whom he thinks will recognise the situation. The main point is that the speaker does not understand what has happened. He can only describe the actual events. It is left to the listener to make the associations, and he eventually provides the words for the speaker's experience.

The author is describing a two-way process. On the one hand, words are shown to be necessary for communicating meaning. They give a form to, as well as expressing experience. Without them one travels through life feeling intensely but understanding nothing. Yet the man who constantly lives within essence, but cannot relate it with formal expression, is actively participating in reality. Without his experience the words would mean nothing. 'A Crazy Tale' comes down slightly on the tall man's side. Essence is still more important than form. But the reader is also left in doubt as to the genuineness of his incomprehensibility. Is it merely a technique to awaken people to the significance of experience? Is it a personal denial of a form that will limit his appreciation? It is these ambiguities that generate the strength of the story.

However, in the transference of his technique of literal reduction from nonsense to exploratory modes, Chesterton has created a problem. Literal levels of words and shapes in nonsense expose the essence. In their structure they are static and closely defined details, indicating logical relationships. Once one invests these levels with formal meaning they may stand for essence but only so far as their limited structure is capable. The approach is adequate for the early nonsense stories. For example in 'A Wild Goose Chase' Chesterton goes from statically indicating the aspects of a man's life in animal figure, to an overall acceptance of the specific essential value of the saying 'a wild goose chase'. These parts and details develop into the use of emblematic characters in 'A Crazy Tale'. The two men have specific functions that make them not valuable in themselves but as emblems whose interaction gives the whole story meaning. There would perhaps have been little problem with the style if the author had continued to write stories primarily concerned with conveying one specific essence. But as the writer tries to integrate form with essence, he is creating a relationship between the two that depends on the reader's experience.

In 'Homesick at Home'[8] he explains the relationship to the reader. The story opens with a paradox: 'The shortest journey from one place to the same place is round the world'; and goes on to present the essential value of experience in understanding words. But it is partly the reader's lack of complete personal experience that weakens the acceptance of the paradox. A great deal of our immediate comprehension of 'A Crazy Tale' is lost in the necessity of viewing the speaker and listener as objects whose meaning has little to do with their individual value as humans because they are emblems. The author's attempt to make the tall man complex as a person whom we can experience results only in confusion. The necessary change and vagary of a human being stand in direct conflict with the emblematic value.

An excellent story showing Chesterton's early grasp of the technical difficulties of portraying experience which is essentially a process, and of an essence which is static, is 'A Picture of Tuesday'. Published in 1896, it was rewritten from an earlier date for *The Quarto*. On an external level, the story is discussing the techniques of impressionism, realism, and symbolism. A group of artists, including

the symbolist Noel Starwood, Staunton the realist, and Oscar
Plumtree as the arbitrary impressionist, come together on a 'subject
day' to compare their pictures of the assigned subject which is
'Tuesday'. Staunton, the realist, has painted a humorous picture of his
mother's 'at home' day which occurred on Tuesdays. The impressionist gives us 'an admirable little suggestion of gaslight in early
morning'. The symbolist has painted a picture of God dividing the
waters on the second day.

What is interesting is the way the symbolic painting communicates. At first it seems to fill the room. The picture's colour is a
labyrinth necessary to follow 'keenly and slowly', when suddenly a
vast human figure is perceived. The logic of the painter must be
understood, and when the initial feeling of vastness is fused with the
knowledge of the form it takes, the reaction is complete. The
experience of the interrelationship of essence and form makes the man
seem to 'rise' with his back towards one, yet the overall response is
definite and absolute: 'It was a dark picture, but when grasped, it
blinded like a sun'. When asked about the inspiration of the painting
Starwood replies that he has to paint something felt as a reality. The
reality is the essence, the inspiration of man. He cannot merely
describe it, he must create an experience of it. He cannot limit this
experience yet he must define it. Consequently there is a relationship
to be perceived and incorporated into a response of feeling, before the
experience and the definition are held in balance. It is indicative of the
early date of the story and Chesterton's less hostile view of
impressionism, that Plumtree is the only one credited with a genuine
understanding of the symbolist's achievement.

In the actual telling of the story Chesterton has, however, not used
the symbol which might have led us to experience rather than just
understand the differences in artistic method. The three artists are
made emblematic from the very first mention of their names. As
emblems the attitudes stand for aspects of art. Staunton represents
form and Plumtree essence, while Starwood is able to balance the
two. Although the author has previously explored the possibility of
words contributing to the expression of value, the exploration was
conducted from the intellectual and almost critical point of view.
When Chesterton tries to put his ideas into practice, he finds himself
still trapped in the vestiges of nonsense that have become emblems.
The use of emblem indicates that he still does not fully trust form to
express essence. Emblem, unlike metaphor, does not replace the thing
that it expresses, but 'stands for' it, stands consciously outside that

object or event inviting comparison with its similarities but not identification. But when words become no longer merely a surface, he has to develop a technique that will stylistically create relationships between the words and the essence.

'A Picture of Tuesday' indicates an early awareness of the fusion of form and essence accomplished by symbol and the metaphors that make it up. Symbols establish a relationship between the word and the object or situation, in which the audience participates. Because symbol creates an experience, the communication that results is concrete and the response is personal. The function of symbol leaves room for growth because of its experiential nature so that form does not limit the essence. For Chesterton experience is paramount in discovering value; yet he also senses a need for definite expression of the essence if it is to resist distortion. The author has to decide whether the individual experience will provide sufficient comprehension or if he must exercise a defining control over the words that will explain them. His awareness that symbolism can create experience, while generating a definite whole, lies behind Chesterton's experiments in 'The Wild Knight'. The poem is important for its attempt to fuse the author's vision of life with a means of expression. However, while he tries to create a work that resolves religious conflict between inspiration and form, and moral conflict between spontaneity and dogma, its success depends on the artistic resolution of definition and experience. Chesterton's attempt to break out of a closely defined emblematic form creates an unresolved stylistic problem. As a result we find an emblematic and symbolic level both working within the poem and coming into conflict with each other.

'The Wild Knight' is difficult to summarise coherently; it is primarily concerned with a poet Redfeather who has to choose between the inspiration of the Wild Knight and the dogma of Lady Olive. The decision is simplified when the anarchist, Lord Oem, kills the Wild Knight and Redfeather after destroying Orm in turn, remains with Lady Olive. The most confusing aspect of the poem is that the title figure, although the most sympathetic character, is not only not the central figure, but also appears to be killed without adequate reason. From another point of view the central figure Redfeather is the least memorable, and is left with an unsatisfactory ending. It is interesting that Redfeather, though weak symbolically, stands in the middle of the emblematic level. If we look at the poem purely as an attempt to define a situation, we recognise that each character stands for a specific essence. The prologue introduces the

Wild Knight as a man of action, close to the direct inspiration of God. The play then opens with the poet Redfeather making explicit the Knight's implied condemnation of corrupt and dogmatic religion. But then he sees Lady Olive leave the church and recognises in her the true and pure aspects of religious guidance. Just as there is a positive and negative side to formal belief, so the opposite of the Knight's inspiration is the anarchy of Lord Orm.

The emblematic level places Redfeather at the centre of the story because he is a poet. He has the artistic problem of balancing inspiration and form. The problem here is that Redfeather is not a clearly defined essence; the story depends on his changing. At the beginning of the poem Redfeather is aware of the negative aspect of form but not of the chaos latent in spontaneity. He begins to understand the chaotic element when he sees Orm's attack on Lady Olive. But it is not until Redfeather has seen Orm destroy the Wild Knight that he is willing to discard the spontaneity altogether. The poet has changed from his initial position and come to think the danger posed by Orm greater than the danger in the dogma of the priests. The reader is left unsatisfied with the result because he is not told why the poet cannot balance the spontaneity and form. Furthermore the artistic imbalance that exists between the symbolic presentation of forces of spontaneity, and the emblematic form of Lady Olive and the priests, deprives Redfeather's choice of credibility.

The ending is also unsatisfactory because there seems to have been no meaning in the Wild Knight's death. Whereas our lack of personal response to Redfeather leaves him vague, our strong sympathy towards the Wild Knight makes his absolute rejection difficult to understand. Again it is the symbolic level in conflict with the emblematic that creates this obscurity because the creation of experience through symbol is responsible for our personal reaction to all the characters, and the Wild Knight is the most vital character in the whole poem.

The problem is that the Knight has to interact continually with the more emblematic functions of the other characters, and the contact undermines his symbolic value. His recognition of Orm as God is weakened by the style of Orm's character. His soliloquy identifies him as anarchy and chaos, believing himself God. But the soliloquy is not static; it is a self-persuasion that ends with the act of burning the title deeds to Olive's house to prove to himself that he does not need human commitments to back up his power. If he can discard his desire for Olive and ignore Redfeather's initial challenge to fight as bonds of human weakness, why does he feel threatened by the Wild Knight? It is only our awareness that Orm's anarchic role is not static that lets us understand his fear that his fantasy will be destroyed by the Wild Knight. The soliloquy by itself may go some way to making the man a symbol; but the reader's constant awareness of the man's emblematic role makes his self-persuasion appear empty and forced, and his killing of the Wild Knight stilted and unnecessary.

The obscurity in style results from an inability to resolve the coexistence of metaphor, which creates experience, with emblem, which defines it. The conflict is one in the author's mind between conscious and unconscious control. His failure to resolve the artistic conflict reflects his failure on a moral and religious level. It shows itself in the opposing methods of the pure man of action and the man of guidance, between the spontaneity of inspiration and the formality of the church. But it is significant that the poet within the poem opts for the only control he can see, that of destruction of the spontaneous, while the author of 'The Wild Knight' opts for conflict between the two. In the next four years we see the author as critic exploring these conflicts. He too comes to opt for control but only when the opposing factors can be both accepted. Finally in *Robert Browning* Chesterton discovered that it was not necessary for spontaneity and form to be in constant conflict. Rather he can place experience and explanation in a balanced tension with each other.

4 Further Confusions: 1904—1907

The resolution of the conflict between experience and explanation that Chesterton found in Browning's poetry, resided in balance: a balance between the conscious and unconscious control of form. But Chesterton soon realised that the resolution was peculiar to Browning; and he moved on in his criticism of 1904—7 to a further search for different modes of expression. Although he now travelled on a more defined path, it is important to keep in mind that during these years the central theme of the total interrelationship between inspiration, life and art, was being transformed into that of the interrelationship of religion, morality and expression.

Several factors lay behind this transformation and one was definitely his marriage to Frances Bloggs who was a devout Anglo-Catholic. Another was his friendship with Hilaire Belloc and gradual acquaintance with Roman Catholicism. But most important was his critical journalistic stance. He soon found that criticising other beliefs and attitudes was ineffective without providing solid reasons for the criticism. As in the Blatchford debate, the reasons became more definite and he gradually found himself defending them. Just as there are theoretical confusions arising from the gradualness of this change, so the vocabulary of the period constantly shifts and contradicts itself.

In 1904 he wrote a book on G. F. Watts. The book presents many sensitive observations on the art of Watts and on that of the nineteenth century as a whole. But despite the overall vision, it is in its detail an immensely confusing work. There appear to be two major arguments: that Watts had a strong sense of artistic responsibility that differentiated him from the aesthetes, and that it was his personal style that conveyed this responsibility. When the details of these two arguments are analyzed Chesterton often appears to undermine his approach by completely contradicting himself.

Initially the critic turned to Watts as a man he greatly admired for his opinions on art, his strong ethical commitment, and his sense of responsibility. But as the book proceeds, it is clear that he is troubled by the artist's style. The problem is that he is looking for the formal resolution that he experiences, yet dislikes the conscious and obvious technique of Watts. As the book progresses from a study of the intent to the style, Chesterton wades through a mass of contradictions before coming to recognise that the valuable communication of the artist is effected by his unconscious style.

The basic intention Chesterton attributes to Watts is his belief 'that he is right'. He has a need to teach 'his internal message and destiny' to others. Since Watts viewed life as a complete whole, it was impossible to separate his art from his ethics, and art became the outlet for his didactic expression. Chesterton calls the artist's abundant confidence in his conscious vision 'universalism'. He notes that it culminates in the belief that Watts never 'doubted that he himself was as central and as responsible as God'; and it is tentatively suggested that universalism may become too individual.

The critic goes on to examine the style in the light of intention. The universalism of Watts's conscious intent demands a universalism of style, a conscious, personal control over the form that is used. To do this the artist never uses current symbols so that his art may not be relegated to the time contemporary with its painting. He has the arrogance to assume that his own symbolic shapes and forms will last longer and communicate more than the collected mythology of the western world. The critic adds that the attempt fails. Here he is concerned to make clear why the attempt fails, stating emphatically that it is not due to the allegorical style but the intent behind it.

Chesterton's discussion of allegory is an important consideration of a form of communication, as well as an explanation for his critical judgement of Watts. The word 'allegory' is used as if it were to painting what symbol is to literature. Watts's pictures are a system unconnected with the effects of words; painting is a language unique to itself. While literature and painting are different media they have similar limitations. Both are arts and more expressive than science. They have no one to one correspondences; and this contributes to their power, but also narrows their limits. Neither can be perfect media for expression, for both communicate only a part of the whole. Watts's painting titled 'Hope' is an example. The title itself communicates a meaning from the unconscious pattern of language, and the picture communicates a part of the truth impossible to put into words. The title and picture are both symbols 'describing another part or aspect of the same complex reality'. While neither expresses perfectly, both express more in the unconscious connections they establish than in their conscious application.

Where Watts fails in Chesterton's eyes, is in consciously thinking that he can perfectly express. Immediately all his pictures are limited to himself. The portrait of Mammon is described as reversing the positions of allegory and reality. Watts has imposed his own idea of reality on it, not giving it the respect due to its actual existence. For this reason Chesterton calls him 'platonic'. He values his idea of the thing more than its actuality; he is a mirror reflecting from himself the values he alone perceives. Ultimately Watts has attempted to paint such pictures 'that no one shall be able to get outside them'. He does so by personally creating the principles by which he paints, and recognising no limits in them for what he wants to say. This limits them to themselves entirely. The chaos the critic experiences looking at this conscious style is a result of its disregard for actuality.

So far Chesterton has discussed the artist's conscious intent and conscious style. However, as he points out in his study of literature and painting, each mode communicates most through its unconscious meaning, and this is finally what is found to be valuable in Watts's pictures. Unfortunately his failure to clarify this point leads to a series of apparent contradictions. Having stated that Watts is didactic — meaning that he has a philosophy to teach — he forgets the 'subtle and unnameable quality' of Watts's worth, and later observes that to be truly didactic is to speak of facts. Art that does this is 'inapplicable to the great needs of man, whether moral or aesthetic'. Having equated the didactic with the purely rationalist, he has equated the teaching of a belief with the wish to convince. Since the critic admires the will to believe but not necessarily the enforcing of belief, he is at cross-purposes with himself. He also makes the error that occurred in 'The Wild Knight' by equating arbitrary, anarchic impulse with spontaneous gesture resulting from inspiration. Elsewhere he considers inspired gesture the basis of ethical behaviour.

What Chesterton is doing is trying to find a balance between the rigid form of the conscious style and formlessness which he mistakenly thinks is part of the unconscious style. He makes similar contradictions when examining the 'mystic and intuitional' link between ethics and art, and saying that there are genuine correspondences between 'a state of morals and an effect in painting'. He concludes that all art communicates an intent. Whistler himself makes a 'sharp and wholesome moral comment' in a streak of yellow paint. In placing the aesthetes with their arbitrariness along with Watts on common ethical ground, he undermines his earlier praise for Watt's unique ethical commitment.

The confusion lies in Chesterton's thinking. We have seen that he believed each man to be directly inspired by God. As such, each man's impressions are equally valid. But the critic has also stated that the artist has a personal responsibility not to leave confusion and vagueness about his inspiration. He is to clarify it through the use of form. Watts would seem to satisfy these criteria. Yet he appears to be condemned when he controls by form; and when he does not use it, he is only on a par with the impressionists, who have no absolute ethical commitment. However, the critic goes on to say that the real difference between Watts and the aesthetes is in the 'nature of the technique'. Considering the pains with which he has demolished the style of Watts's painting, it is at first hard to appreciate the value that difference will make. In the last part of the book the division between the conscious and unconscious style is recognised and defined by the author and it partially resolves the confusion.

The final section comments on an unconscious inspiration from an external source in the colour and line of Watts's style. These aspects are the techniques of the spontaneous man who has a definite belief in an external power. Therefore the style is not arbitrary unconscious formlessness but externally guided form. The techniques communicate directly and clearly to the viewer. Chesterton finishes the book saying:

> I believe that often he has scarcely known what he is doing; I believe that he has been in the dark when the lines came wrong; that he has been still deeper in the dark and things came right . . . His automatic manual action is . . . certainly a revelation to himself . . . his right hand has taught him terrible things. (169)

What Chesterton has found in Watts is that he cannot achieve an artistic balance consciously. His consciously spontaneous form results in impressionism and his controlled intent produces didactic rationalism. Both limit and sever the expression from actual things. Subconsciously, however, Watts communicates the inspiration of God, and this is his valuable moral teaching. There is an implication that this 'subconscious' style should really be conscious if the intent is to measure up to artistic responsibility. It is only because there is no conscious indication of God that the weight of maintaining the balance between spontaneity and control is thrown onto the human powers alone. Unfortunately the limitations of man make it impossible to sustain such a balance.

Despite its confusions *G. F. Watts* added to Chesterton's reputation and probably increased the attention being paid to his essays. At this time the author was leading a demanding journalistic career but without much financial success. His next book *Heretics* was at least partially an attempt to make some money out of the sale of a collection of his newspaper articles. As such it is a reflection of his varied life at this time, yet it is also a major critical assessment of some of his contemporaries in which he studies further the thin line that man must walk between impressionism and rationalism.

Although several of the articles were rewritten for the book, the essays are essentially independent statements given a framework in the first and last entries. While the form gives little direction, the difficulty with the book lies far deeper. The critic wants first to examine the superior qualities of contemporary didactic writers, whom he now calls 'dogmatic', over the aesthetes and the scientists; yet he also wants to criticise the individual dogmas. The potential confusion is increased when the critic argues for the importance of the dogmatist's popular literary success, yet adds that he is not as interested in their 'merely literary manner' as in their ideas. The essays as a whole create an unavoidable feeling that the criticism of the ideas originates in criticism of the literary styles.

Ironically the confusion in Chesterton's argument is both created and controlled by his wonderful critical confidence. If he feels something to be wrong in any particular writer yet cannot rationally explain what it is, he invariably uses an amusing anecdote or phrase to create the 'attitude' he wants. The reader is guided through the work not by consistent argument but by a marvellous sense of humour that certainly appears to go right to the heart of each matter. This method later becomes essential to Chesterton's style; it works by creating in the reader a response analogous to the writer's own. But whereas the later style is based on reasonable, if not rational argument, here the fundamental criteria are obscured. The humour makes possible an evasion of straightforward critical judgement. However, this confusion is partially resolved by the broad structure of the work, which points out to the reader areas that Chesterton was later to explore.

Despite this problem *Heretics* does clarify the confusion between didactic and rational that existed in *G. F. Watts* by using the word 'dogma'. Dogma is presented as originating in the primal inspiration of the spontaneous man. An initial belief once defended, is defined, clarified and made dogmatic. As Chesterton himself knew, 'Truths turn into dogmas the instant they are disputed'. The claim for inspiration lends much greater weight to the attack on the aesthetic art of the period, because it establishes a basis common to both dogmatist and aesthete. What each does with the inspiration becomes the question. The differences between the two in Chesterton's eyes is that the dogmatist has standards and the aesthete does not. It is the limitation that a man forces on himself that gives him the ability to go further, and Chesterton is arguing that a work based on dogma and ethical standards will be stylistically and artistically better because of the definitions the artist is aware of.

The central essays of the book examine specific proponents of aesthetic theories from the perspective of the separation of art and morals. It is important to remember that for Chesterton 'moral' means all God-inspired action. The aesthete's belief that emotion originates in self leads him to think that he personally can control it completely. He recognises no external value in actual things because he invests them completely with his own. George Moore is criticised along with Walter Pater because 'his real quarrel with life is that it is not a dream that can be moulded by the dreamer'. Moore is so self-centred that he does not even have the unconscious revelation of Watts. The critic concludes that egoism cuts off revelation and genuine inspiration; it is, 'not merely a moral weakness, it is a very constant and influential aesthetic weakness as well'.

The moral weakness derives from the separation of art from external inspiration. Chesterton has always believed that art is indivisibly connected with morality. It is the human expression of a divine inspiration. Because the aesthetes suggest that the two are mutually exclusive, they conclude that morality need not enter art. Chesterton's view is that they are just not aware of the morals they live from day to day. He thinks that the difference between the aesthetes and the dogmatists lies in the conscious awareness of the latter of inspiration and specific belief. While similar to the aesthetes in always thinking themselves right, they are willing to state their beliefs. They have a bias against other people's morality yet they are consciously aware of specific points of difference. However the case for the dogmatists is weakened by Chesterton's criticism of the dogmas themselves. He bases it in the one fundamental similarity existing between the aesthetes and dogmatists: the central role of the self.

The contemporaries Chesterton chooses to assess are Wells, Kipling and Shaw. Wells is praised for his continual growth; yet is condemned for his denial of standards. Kipling is praised for seeing the wonder of everyday life; yet is condemned for reducing courage, valour and belief to obedience, duty and discipline. Lastly Shaw is admired for his thorough and just consistency; yet is condemned for the belief that he saw things as they really were and that 'the golden rule was that there was no golden rule'.

In each case the man is condemned for the personal and relative aspect of his work. The critic shows each dogmatist denying the existence of dogma; but this is no paradox, merely a failure to clarify vocabulary and thought. Chesterton fully respects each man for his conscious ethical standards, yet he cannot reconcile them with a growing conviction of the existence of an absolute moral standard. The final chapter asserts that if there is to be mental growth 'it must mean the growth into more and more definite convictions, into more and more dogmas'. Yet in the same chapter he says that he cannot justify the existence of a large number of dogmas, he can only admire the conviction behind them. While a perfectly tenable position, it is his failure to clarify the difference between relative ethics and absolute morality that is the source of the confusion. The recognition of an unknowable absolute is the one thing Chesterton notes as lacking in the dogmas of these men. Without it there is always the danger of forgetting the external and becoming impressionist.

Although the dangers are less emphasised than in *G. F. Watts*, the critic also relates the opinions of the dogmatists to scientific rationalism. Where the rationalists fail is in their unwillingness to admit that there is something that exists beyond their system; for, like the aesthetes, they are self-centred. In one essay Chesterton comments that, 'the man of science, not realising the ceremonial is essentially a thing done without reason, has to find a reason for every sort of ceremonial'; yet 'like all the important emotions of human existence, it is essentially irrational'. He notes that paganism believed in total intellectual comprehension, but that after Christianity their 'naked innocence of the intellect' was shown to be misleading. Christianity revealed the concept of mysticism and intuition. Although Chesterton carefully distinguishes between the rationalist who argues from pre-established rules, and the dogmatist who argues from personal belief, the similarity of their explaining of ideas through rational argument brings them close together. Just as the dogmatist is always close to aesthetic impressionism, so also is he in danger of rationalism if he fails to acknowledge the unknowable absolute.

The dogmatists are not totally spontaneous because they have definite opinions, and they are not totally rational because of their belief in an unknown. Yet because they do not use a style which consciously indicates God, the artistic balance devolves upon themselves and they are continually slipping off into one extreme or the other. Their conscious and unconscious styles are not as radically divergent as those of G. F. Watts, but their insistence on personal opinions and standards denies the admitting of their unconscious inspiration into their art. Finally, Chesterton's criticism of the dogmatists originates from a fault of their literary styles.

Despite Chesterton's stated intention of discussing ideas rather than literary form, the central group of essays does concentrate on style. If we remember the final acknowledgement of the value in Watts's unconscious communication that succeeded in revealing the inexpressible, the study of ritual and ceremony in *Heretics* is an inevitable development. Immediately the initial discussion of dogmatism finishes, Chesterton inserts a curious essay called 'Christmas and the Aesthetes'. It takes a look at both the Salvation Army and Comtism from the point of view of distinguishing between their aims and their methods. While faulting the aims of both, the critic praises their recognition of the need for ritual. Ritual not only satisfied the need for conscious control by indicating an external standard in the form, but also satisfies the need for spontaneous inspiration since the indicated external eludes rational comprehension.

The controlling value of ritual is that it attempts to get closer to absolute expression by acting directly rather than communicating in language. Chesterton's earlier anxieties over the imperfection of language in *G. F. Watts* are beginning to crystallise. Action, and dance the artistic form of it, become important to expression; and interestingly enough the critic links both with the use of paradox in literature. One of the last essays of the book specifically states that humanity is divided into conscious and unconscious ritualists, and that the conscious form is far more admirable because it indicates a choice of the will. The critic goes on to say that religious ritual is not the mere secular, passing symbol of a white bow tie and tails required by the unconscious ritual of a dinner table. The use of religious ritual is humbling. It admits the impossibility of perfect human expression. It admits further a personal weakness in the face of the mythical symbols of the world. It acknowledges the existence of an external power. Although the connection is never formally made, the

presence of many essays on ritual in a book about dogma suggests that
ritual may supply what these dogmatists lack. Ritual acknowledges
the unchanging in its formality, yet allows change in its admission of
human limitations.

Although a discussion of ritual is present in the book, it is not a
major part of Chesterton's argument. Fundamentally, what he is
examining is the danger of aestheticism. While he confuses the issue
by failing to differentiate between aesthetic ethics and dogmatic
morals, the emphasis lies on the need to communicate beliefs as
opposed to having a non-committal aesthetic attitude. What is
admirable about the dogmatists is their control, their conscious
communication of opinion that acts as an overall net against
vagueness and irresponsibility. Chesterton likes them because they
guard against the potential anarchy of the mind. On the whole,
however, the criticism is negative. It points out the curative effects of
dogmatism and does not see it as preventative. The stress is on what it
does not do, rather than what it does.

The negative approach of his criticism is also evident in
Chesterton's newspaper articles written between 1904 and 1907. As
with the earlier group of essays, these follow a pattern of gradual
change. Despite the yield of an inevitable mountain of mundane
observation, they present an unique opportunity to assess the currents
of the time and how they affected the development of one of its
profound thinkers. It must be stated again that such an assessment can
only note the shifts in the emphasis of such thought — especially since
Chesterton commented infrequently on himself and his work, and
does so only through his comments on others. The essays contain
common elements reaching back to his earliest work, but the year
1907 does seem to crystallise these elements into a sudden confidence.
This is mainly due to the successful transforming of his vocabulary
into religion, morality and expression through his acceptance of the
Anglo-Catholic church in *Orthodoxy* which was written in 1907.

A result of the necessary process of clarification following from his
critical discussions about the beliefs of others, was a lessening in the
number of essays making generalised comments about religion.
Perhaps realising that his own beliefs were not entirely definite, the
critic turned instead to commenting on the aspects that he knew he
disliked. Modern religions are criticised for being negative, for
concentrating on the virtues of avoidance rather than the positive
morality of conscious attempt. Furthermore, a necessary result of
having to clarify his position was the realisation that he had certain

beliefs that formed a dogmatic standpoint. Although for some time
he does not appear to differentiate between the value of personal
ethics and of formal, organised religion recognising an absolute
morality.

Chesterton continues to consider the value of the actual world as
imperative to morality. There is a need to guard against a self-centred
standard of behaviour because it does not respect the existence of
others. There is also no such thing as a private morality. During 1906
a new note is sounded in an essay called 'The Wind and the Trees'.[1]
The form of the piece is parable. In it Chesterton denies the influence
of merely material circumstances on morals. He adds that man not
only has the right to recognise an external origin of moral standards,
but also the duty to resist subversion of those standards by material
demands. In 1907 the ideas become more defined, and the critic
moves away from purely personal ethics towards absolute morality.
He notes that 'a man's minor actions and arrangements ought to be
more free, flexible, creative; the things that should be unchangeable
are his principles, his ideals'.[2] Morality begins to be seen as something
external to man and absolute; the critic speaks of 'right as existing
outside human weakness and without reference to human error'.[3]

The function of art as an expression of morality becomes unclear
during this period because of the linguistic confusion between ethics
and morals. All art, because it is created by people with individual
opinions and standards may incorporate those opinions and reflect
their ethical standpoint. But sometimes a person has an absolute
moral standard in addition to this ethical commitment and his art may
also contain a moral statement. The difference between the relative
and personal basis for ethics and the absolute and external basis for
morals, means that while all art may be ethical, not all art may be
moral. But one thing is certain, as Chesterton's consciousness of
morality grows, so does his theme of artistic responsibility.

Once more the year 1907 produces a more defined concept of the
function of art. With the acknowledgement of an external authority,
and an absolute morality, the artist has a highly responsible role. Art
must establish limits to experience, and these limits are the human
perceptions of the existence of an absolute. Art and religion are now
connected in a far more specific way than they were in the earlier
criticism. Both concentrate on detail which provides definition:
'poetry and religion always insist upon the proximity, the almost
menacing closeness of the things with which they are concerned'.[4]
Both are concerned with clarity of vision. Chesterton singles out

romance as being similar to religion in that they both have a goal. They both 'see everything as it were foreshortened . . . and it is the whole essence of perspective that it comes to a point'.[5] Yet he is still concerned with inspiration, and says that romance also contains within itself the possibility of inspiration that transcends these limits. The inspiration of art is as valuable as the limiting function. Indeed the function of art is both to limit and inspire; but the author no longer looks for a form to balance the two, but for one that will combine them.

In 1905 the balance of the two aspects of experience and explanation is still present in Chesterton's concept of form. However, there is a far greater emphasis on the limiting role, which no doubt arises from his growing belief in dogma. Two essays written in 1905[6] indicate an understanding of the difference between the rationalistic and the dogmatic. The early respect for heraldry is acknowledged to be ultimately too limiting since like other sciences heraldry depends heavily on the process of rational logic. The critic points out that logic is not a thing, not even an abstract thing; it is merely a didactic process. Rationalism is useful to dogma, but without the initial inspiration in dogma, it is worthless. The second essay notes the importance of ceremony to express these truths that logical processes like speech cannot communicate. The essay continues by saying that 'ceremony begins where dogma leaves off'. In the former essay logic and reason are not rejected insofar as they are useful, but Chesterton is pointing out that there are things they cannot express. Similarly in the second there is no rejection of dogma or humanly limited explanation of belief, only an acknowledgement that to communicate the inspiration behind it needs a ceremonial form of expression.

In the following year the reader finds an increasing anxiety over the arbitrariness of language as an expressive mode. Again a linguistic problem arises when Chesterton uses words like simile and metaphor, or symbol and fantasy interchangeably. However, the content of the essays is clear. In his column for the *Illustrated London News* the critic replies to a reader's question saying:

> I thought of metaphor being dangerous because it was a good metaphor . . . Nobody remembers that a simile is never quite right, that there is always some point where a simile is wrong.[7]

Another essay notes that abstract terms are 'really most concrete'. They make no pretence to being the thing they represent, yet they stand for the closest that a man comes to representing that thing. The argument continues by observing that metaphors are different. A metaphor is the assumption of another identity that pretends to be what it represents. Since this is impossible in absolute terms, the meaning of the object represented will be shifted if one thinks of the metaphor as real.

Chesterton at this time seems to have come to an impasse. He still acknowledges that an artist is exercising a divine aspect of his nature in creating. Yet it seems impossible for the artist to express without imposing his own arbitrary personal perception on the objects he discusses. The earlier references to ceremony indicated that it lay beyond 'the reason and the tongue'; but the critic seems to be breaking through to a new conception of ritual. As we shall see in the critical work *Charles Dickens*, Chesterton arrives at the idea of the artist as one who uses forms of ritual to express himself, because ritual indicates both human limits and what lies beyond. The development into a full scheme of allegorical writing does not occur until 1912; but the essays of 1907 discussed here introduce the origins of the idea.

To understand 'ritual' we should return to Chesterton's respect for actuality. We find that it has become a bulwark against arbitrary expression. As essay on medieval illustrations observes that:

all these pictures are designed to express things in their quiddity . . . Their [medieval artists'] pencils often go wrong as to how the thing looks; their intellects never go wrong as to what the thing is. [8]

The important point is not to let personal perceptions of an object interfere with what it really is. The result of such interference is that the objects decay into the aspects one wants to see. In terms of form, 'to see a thing in aspects is to be crippled, to be defective . . . This is the thing called "impressionism"'. But what specific form one can employ to avoid this arbitrary nature still eludes him. He notes elsewhere that 'material metaphors' make clear what they represent. Further they admit that they represent rather than become the object, and simultaneously communicate the limits of the artist's expression. In an essay concerning the difference between clear and arbitrary symbols the critic uses a different vocabulary to observe:

all reasonable men believe in symbol; but some reasonable men do

not believe in ritualism; by which they mean, I imagine, a
symbolism too complex, elaborate, and mechanical.[9]

He goes on to point out that 'religious forms are, at the worst, fables:
they might be true. Secular forms are falsehoods; they are not true'.
By 'secular' is meant images in which the meanings of words have
become associative and unprecisely used although they imply direct
communication; they say one thing while meaning another. Religious forms express something that cannot be directly communicated; but they do not pretend to do so fully themselves.

The function of ritual is therefore religious. It enables man to
express divine inspiration, but makes clear his human limitations.
Specifically it makes necessary the use of obvious images that indicate
rather than become objects. The writer must not impose his personal
perception on the images; they must communicate for him. An
important aspect is that the form does not balance inspiration and
control but lets them exist simultaneously under an unknown
external. One form that Chesterton turns to as an example is the fairy-
tale. Although there was a growing contemporary awareness of their
importance he was one of the first to recognise that the tales were a
kind of archetype for existence. This opinion stands out clearly
against many contemporaries who said that fairy-tales were anti-
social and could pervert children. The critic praises them specifically
because of their morality which is based on a combination of rigid
promises or laws, and unknowable magic or God. By 1907 fairy-tales
are seen as a form of ceremony, of ritual. One knows that they are not
literally 'true'; yet through their inclusion of both limitation and
magic they communicate the external inspiration for the laws by
which they operate, and thereby validate the existence they express.
However, these early forays appear to be only tentative solutions to
the problem of the responsibility of the artist, as the reservations
about them in *Charles Dickens* shows.

Coming to year 1906 and the book *Charles Dickens*, we find
Chesterton approaching the end of three years of critical struggle.
The contradictions and revelations it contains illustrate the impasse he
had reached concerning the nature of the artist, and some faint
indications of a way out. In turning to Dickens Chesterton was
turning to a writer who had obviously fascinated him for some time.
He had already written a considerably perceptive essay on the novelist
in a Bookman Booklet of 1903, as well as several newspaper articles.
Also by this time in Chesterton's career, the two men had some

fundamental stylistic elements in common. They both produced caricatures of people; they both had the journalistic habit of writing to a set length that creates pulses of movement through a book; and most of all they both used exaggeration in an original and creative manner. It is perhaps because of these similarities that the examination of Dickens and the study of his proposed lapse of responsibility in the later work, becomes a study of Chesterton's fears for himself as a writer and artist.

At the time, the importance of *Charles Dickens* must have been that it consolidated Chesterton's critical career. The book splits Dickens's career into the now well-recognised early and late styles of writing. The early style is portrayed as a form of conscious fantasy, while the later is called an attempt at realism. The major element of the earlier style is exaggeration, which Chesterton calls 'the definition of art'. Of Dickens's work as a whole, the critic says that 'Dickens did not strictly make a literature; he made a mythology'. By mythology he means folklore, and the study of Dickens as a folklorist shows his growing interest in the fairy-tale as a form of ritual. The reader is told that fairy-tales can communicate the unknowable and indefinable by acknowledging limits in order to go beyond them. The critic also stresses the suggestion that folklore provides an instinct of something enduring beyond its episodes, 'The characters are felt to be fixed things of which we have fleeting glimpses; that is, they are felt to be divine'.

The presence of limitation and inspiration is transcended in Dickens's early works. Chesterton attributes the brilliance of the characterisations to an ability to find the vast yet unchanging essence of a person; and then create the physical limits of a human being around it. The reader knows that the physical appearance of the character is connected to essence by the transcendent truth of his soul. Although there is a necessary and active sense of personal creation on Dickens's part, the consciousness of this fantasy constantly acknowledges the external and absolute truth that lies beyond it, and the fantasy performs a moral function by clarifying this truth. In fantasy and its exaggeration Dickens ritualises something he cannot fully express.

However, Chesterton warns that the incomplete recognition of the external sometimes misleads Dickens. When the novelist does not understand, the exaggerations can go too far. There are details:

which he endows with a demonic life. The things seem more actual

than they really are. Indeed, that degree of realism does not exist in
reality: it is the unbearable realism of a dream. (47)

When the author forgets that his fantasy is only fantasy, only a limit,
he becomes despotic; and the objects he describes lose their connection with reality and truth. Similarly, the recognition of limits
which leads Dickens to a taste for literary frameworks can devolve
into 'room within room of some labyrinthine but comfortable castle'.
When he forgets the external truth and becomes despotic he tries to
overcompensate his characters by making them too comfortable.
Chesterton insists that 'something more than this is needed from the
man who is imagining and making men, the artist'. The disintegration into despotic fantasy destroys the truly creative function of the
artist which always acknowledges the existence of an external
inspiring absolute.

Having praised yet criticised the early style of Dickens, the critic
moves on to the later style. The condemnation of realism in the later
works rests on the statement that 'Art copies life in not copying life,
for life copies nothing'. As Dickens becomes careful of exact
construction in art, his wish to construct reality exactly grows.
Chesterton bewails the fact that the novelist believed that realism was
showing things 'as they are', or reproducing. The critic's own view
was that a communication of essence was as fully real as the artist
could be, for all perceptions of appearance are only partial. He
concludes that Dickens 'denied his own divine originality, and
pretended he had plagiarised from life'. The author who does this
forgets the boundaries of human expression and the limiting function
of art. Any attempt to express life without the acknowledgement of
the illusion, will fail. As a result the realism of the later work is seen as
a falling away from the communication of truth, even though the
author becomes technically more experienced and careful.

At this point the reader is faced with a serious problem. The
creative side of Dickens was shown to become too creative and
degenerate into despotic fantasy. The imitative side of Dickens was
shown to fail because of the impossibility of perfect reproduction.
Yet, the critic condemns the styles for what they say about the man
not about the artist, and therefore separates his judgement of the man
from that of the art. The idea is totally alien to all his thinking and
implies that there is one standard for art and another for life. It may be
because of this 'unnatural' separation that Chesterton demonstrates a
definite sense of uncertainty in *Charles Dickens* despite brilliant

judgements of individual aspects of Dickens's work.

Chesterton greatly admired Dickens's writing, yet could not reconcile this with the fact that certain aspects of the works left him distinctly uncomfortable. What the critic condemns is the despotic fantasy and the realism, yet he does not coherently explain why. From his comments it is evident that he objects primarily to the assertion of personal opinion to the exclusion of external authority, or the assertion of an individual ethic over absolute morality. But Chesterton himself does not seem to be consciously aware that this is the criterion for his judgement. He admires the great artistic skill of the personally dominated work but dislikes the view of the world that it implies. Instead of realising that this tension is a direct result of ethically based art, he assumes that there are two standards present; and makes his assessment of both work and man highly ambiguous.

In *Robert Browning* the tension between the external and the personal was that between dogma and inspiration. Now this tension can no longer exist because dogma has been shown to originate in inspiration. The two together form the basis of a man's behaviour. The distinction between morality and ethics was doubly unnecessary to make in *Robert Browning* because the form already acknowledged an external authority. But the failure to make the distinction resulted in the confusion of Chesterton's following critical works. In *G. F. Watts* Chesterton excused the conscious personal ethics by pointing to the clear, externally inspired, moral message of the unconscious style. *Heretics* criticised the dogmatists for not indicating in style the unexplainable external moral standard of their dogmas. Now in *Charles Dickens* we see that the critic separates art from life if the art only reflects personal standards. As a result he condemns the form of realism that claims personal authority, and applauds the folklore which admits the existence of an external authority and inspiration. But here as in the earlier books Chesterton's failure to clarify his meaning obscures the process of his thought, and the value of his work. What should be noted is that the critic's stress on personal control as a means of avoiding impressionism has shifted to become a stress on the indication of external inspiration to avoid the personal despotic perversion of actual things. Furthermore the negative criticism of the earlier works is giving way to a more positive approach. Both changes are due to Chesterton's finding of a form which satisfied his expressive requirements.

Charles Dickens is also a document of personal exploration, and the fundamental question of an artist's responsibility to absolute standards is subtly, even unconsciously, established in the correlation between Chesterton's reference to himself as a critic and Dickens as an artist. The initial paragraphs of the book introduce us to Chesterton as critic. They are at first bewildering in their apparently unconnected discussion of the meaning of words. Not until one completes the book does one realise their full application. The critic begins by making the distinction between the unknowable absolute and the arbitrary.

> Much of our modern difficulty, in religion and other things, arises merely from this: that we confuse the word 'indefinable': with the word 'vague'. (1)

The difference between the two is that 'indefinable' means 'the first thing; the primary fact', the actuality, the essence of an object. While 'vague' means loose, impressionistic, carelessly expressed. Having applied 'indefinable' to the spirit, to a man, he now applies it to 'the word'; 'the word that has no definition is the word that has no substitute'. The critic now goes on to apply the word 'great' to Dickens; yet makes it clear that he cannot explain the term, he can only use it. It is doubtful that such a generous author as Chesterton would involve himself in this elaborate word-play merely to defend himself against having to explain himself. He appears to be making a general statement about his limitations as a critic. The limitations are exactly those he sees in the early Dickens who uses his original creativity to express a further essence that cannot be defined.

Chesterton recognises a similarity between what he does and what the artist does. Just as the artist uses art to express and recreate the experience of life, so the critic uses an art in criticism to express and recreate the experience of art. It is probably not coincidence, but more a natural association of thought that makes the critic speak of his own limits immediately after a chapter on those of the artist. The condemnation of the later Dickens who attempts to imitate life 'in cataloguing the facts of life', is followed in the next chapter by the statement that the critic cannot tell us everything and that he professes only to give 'an opinion or a summary deducible from the facts'. A more explicit correlation is made when Chesterton tries finally to assess his subject. He complains that criticism of a creative mode like art is a staggering responsibility similar to that of the philosopher or artist in his interpretation and expression of life, and that to criticise adequately he needs, 'religion or, at least, a dogmatic philosophy'. If one continues the correlation between the artist and critic, the implication is that just as the critic must have some external religious philosophy, so the artist must have some absolute moral basis if he is to create valuable art.

Finally, Chesterton sees in Dickens both the positive and negative aspects of his own inseparably connected life and art. He knows that Dickens as creator 'did not point out things, he made them'. In doing so he exercised his half-divine origins. Yet the criticism of the book has indicated the ease with which human desire for power takes over and attempts to claim creation purely for itself. Chesterton instantly recognises this as the first step towards solipsism and denounces it as a moral failure that negates the value of the art. In different words, it is the replacement of moral standards by ethical. The critic on the other hand only points out the meaning of an event, and is never in danger of attempting absolute personal creation. The parallels the author constructs between himself as critic and Dickens as artist appear as an assessment of the critic against the artist. In all the things that Chesterton values most the two roles correspond. They differ only in that the critic does not presume to create *ex nihilo*; he has a permanent sense of his inadequacy in comparison to the reality he examines. The difference will become very important as Chesterton comes to see the potential despotism of the artist as more dangerous.

5 Mapping the Artistic Terrain: 1904—1907

The poem 'The Wild Knight' contained a radical divergence between Chesterton's style and the apparent meaning of his story. The style indicated a conflict between the conscious control of the writer through emblem, and the unconscious control that allowed for spontaneity within metaphor. However, the content of the poem implied that spontaneity had to be destroyed completely in order to avoid the danger of anarchy and chaos. At the root of this division lay an inability to differentiate between a personal spontaneity, advocated by Lord Orm, and an externally inspired spontaneity, as found in the Wild Knight. The author recognised the positive value of the Wild Knight, and the decision to destroy him contradicts this awareness. Yet the conflict in the style indicates an intuitive knowledge that something is unbalanced.

The early criticism shows Chesterton asking the artist to walk on a thin line between control and spontaneity. The identification of personal and external inspiration as one left the artist in constant danger of slipping either into arbitrary impression or rational argument. The main discovery of the subsequent criticism was that control and inspiration were impossible to balance; human judgement alone could not do it. Once the critic begins to recognise an external authority he takes his first step towards the destination of his style, which is allegory; he realises that impressions may not be inspired, they may be personal only. Similarly didacticism may become personal despotism. The existence of a self-centred basis of non-inspired work provided him with a partial solution. Previously the artist had verged on the blasphemy of being God if he tended either to impressionism or rationalism. Chesterton now states that while art is still an absolute necessity for a human being, it is only valuable if consciously inspired by God. The artist's recognition of the presence of God in the work will effect the balance between spontaneity and control and the corresponding connection between essence and form. The idea is reached primarily in *Robert Browning*.

One of the important conclusions of that work was that the style was instrumental in the necessary expression of the presence of God. *Robert Browning* becomes a landmark in Chesterton's work not only because it recognises a necessity for the presence of God, but also because it initiates the search for an adequate style to fulfil that need.

Following close on *Robert Browning* is Chesterton's first novel, *The Napoleon of Notting Hill*. Here the search for style is translated into a confrontation between the artist of the self and the artist of external inspiration. The message conveyed is that the conscious and unconscious control they exercise in emblem and metaphor respectively, can co-exist. Not only can they co-exist but also if they do co-exist, they create the ultimate form for human expression. Because emblem is personally based it may always lose the balance between form and essence. Yet despite the value of metaphor with its ability to communicate external inspiration through experience, Chesterton does not entirely trust it because of its experiential character which is open to misinterpretation. Emblem is more closely allied to explanation. It is shown to provide the conscious control metaphor lacks, and metaphor the external basis that emblem does not have. However, in practice the two together do not make an adequate form. The author himself senses this and opts for conscious emblematic control over the whole novel, with the exception of a few sections which attempt to incorporate metaphor. He thinks that although metaphor is a more valuable form of expression, it is also more dangerous if it fails. The novelist's expression is further stabilised by the extensive use of explanation to prevent misinterpretation of either form.

The novel takes place 80 years in the future when London is governed by a huge bureaucracy headed by a randomly selected despot. The action begins with the selection of a new despot, the artist Auberon Quin. He proceeds to enforce a personal joke on the town by re-instituting the old medieval boroughs, with all their customs and costumes. The bureaucracy is annoyed by this intervention, but because the joke does not interfere with the actual functioning of London they tolerate its existence. Ten years later, however, a young man called Adam Wayne appears who takes the joke seriously. As provost of Notting Hill, he refuses to let the other London boroughs run a road through the centre of his territory. He objects because of a patriotic dedication to Notting Hill and is prepared to live up to the conditions of Quin's joke by fighting for the territory's freedom. Such seriousness infects the other provosts and a war breaks out, resulting in the victory of Wayne and the Empire of Notting Hill.

Chesterton's tight control renders the story highly schematic. The characters have obvious and clearly defined emblematic roles. Auberon Quin is the personal artist, the aesthete working from his own impressions and consciously controlling them. Adam Wayne is the artist dependent on external inspiration and unconscious control through metaphor. The bureaucratic masses are represented by Barker, the non-artist, the man who cannot perceive any connection between expression and meaning. As an impressionist, the forms Quin thinks up are related only to himself. He does not believe in value that is not generated by his own ideas. Hence he sees no connection between form and essence. In fact he denies the existence of essence outside of his own perspective. The method of this art is to create emblems, or forms that stand for an object, and impose them on surroundings things. The mode is really a form of nonsense logic in that the intent is always to shatter the existence of 'normal' logic; and it has the same effects. The first effect is that it disorients one's usual response to the object; and the second is that it defines the response in the terms imposed by the artist.

The novelist indicates both the positive and negative value in these effects. After Quin is made King, he receives Barker in an audience. Immediately, he asks for Barker's hat which Barker hands over. Quin then sits on the hat saying that it is a 'quaint old custom'. Barker can see no logic in the nonsense. He cannot understand why Quin would want to create a 'custom' and is soon reduced to frantic walking back and forth. The unrelated forms Quin creates have the parodic function of nonsense. They strip away convention in order to reveal essence, only to reveal that there is no essence. Yet if the people cannot appreciate the intent, the disorientation of nonsense becomes purely arbitrary and unrelated, and is therefore dismissed as chaotic, and the imposition of his definitions is objected to as dogmatic.

The disorientation by nonsense through emblem is intended by Quin to destroy convention. It assumes that there is no essence to be revealed, and that there is no absolute meaning. As a result the emblem is easily misunderstood and reduced to didacticism and impressionism. If, however, the emblems do stand for an essence, which Quin does not believe, the disorientation reveals new aspects of meaning; and the imposed definitions become constructive forms within which to live. Adam Wayne takes the red uniform of Notting Hill seriously. He is not aware of the destructive satiric function of Quin's joke. The emblems become metaphors for him; they are inseparable from the inspiration of his life. He says 'I would paint the Red Lion on my shield if I had only my blood'.

The author calls Wayne a 'dumb poet', a man who normally expresses his inspiration in action. But Wayne has been born into a world where the form for expressing his inspiration exists in the medieval emblems of Quin; and through them he can communicate his inspiration to other people. Wayne employs the emblems as metaphors by insisting that they are at one with the object for which they stand. Metaphorical form recreates experience by fusing the actual with inspired expression. It cannot be simply dismissed as arbitrary definition since it claims to contain essence within it, and it demands involvement in the experience on the audience's part. The positive aspects of his expression are that he creates an experience of essence and causes an individual reassessment of meaning. But this depends upon the success of communication. If the connection between form and essence is not understood, his expression will appear to lack inspiration and relapse into the dangers of rationalism and impressionism. The negative effect of Wayne's metaphors which necessitate involvement are far more serious than Quin's arbitrary emblems that can be dismissed as chaotic. The experiencing of something unknown is frightening and terrible, and the negative aspects of metaphor exist in this potential for creating fear that destroys all sense of order.

Wayne manages to communicate momentarily his inspiration to Quin. The full force of essence beyond his emblems at first disorients Quin, just as his emblems disoriented Barker. He calls Wayne a mad man, just as he has been called mad. When he fully understands he is almost convinced of a view 'so desperate — so responsible'. Yet he will not allow himself to experience Wayne's essence. To do so would destroy his attempt at total personal control.

Quin, Wayne and Barker are portrayed emblematically by the novelist in that he does not change their basic nature. He himself curtails the negative effects of emblem by employing extensive explanations. The terms he uses do not ask for experience; the characters are presented to stand for modes of expression. Barker's 'bleak blue eyes', and his favourite expression 'speaking in the interests of the public', are constants throughout the book. When he is described 'flinging up his fingers with a feverish American move-ment' or walking with 'his frock-coat flapping like the black wings of a bird', the observations do not create an experience of Barker. Rather, they indicate the attitude of the novelist to the character; they are subtle explanations on his part. Quin is portrayed in a quietly satirical vein. The reader's reaction is an appreciation of the author's humour, of the point the author is making on Quin's external communication; he does not react to Quin himself. Similarly the chapter devoted to the 'Mental Condition of Adam Wayne' carefully builds up an explanation for his perceptions, actions and reactions. The novelist presents his characters so they cannot be radically misunderstood, and he makes sure that they continue to stand for the values with which he imbues them.

The conscious control extends to the tight structural movement of the book. The opening chapter establishes the 'cheat the prophet' action which underlies the serial progression of the chapters. The novelist's contemporaries have dared to try to predict the future; and he ridicules this as impossible. The book presents a sequence of the three static modes of expression each succeeding the other. The five sections of the book each contain three chapters that examine a point of view, show it in action, and lead to its change. The sequence leads finally to the last chapter which is quite different in tone. It contains the union of Wayne and Quin, and elevates them from the dual pattern of meaning the novel has followed. The author recognises the inadequacy of the child vision in the central novel; by itself it is closely connected with the childish joke of Quin. Yet the adult vision of the first chapter of purely rational prophets predicting static futures, is also inadequate. The control makes clear the recognition of the three static characters, the sequential structure culminating in union, and the significant difference in the function of the last chapter. However, a full appreciation of the value of the novel is dependent on the individual response the reader gives to the metaphorical skill of the author.

In *G. F. Watts* Chesterton says that style is at its best when it is shown to correspond with internal meaning. Unless it is purely a technical exercise there must be some connection between form and essence. Although the novelist recognises the dangers of metaphor, he also realises that it is necessary because it connects form and essence. At a few significant points he creates a metaphorical depth to the characters which yields a carefully confined transcendent meaning for the book. There are few consistent metaphors that become symbols, but there are metaphorically created actions and events. These are concentrated in the parts where the modes of expression of the characters come into contact.

An initial example is the introduction of Quin as he walks to work behind two men in frock-coats. The transformation of the coats into dragons indicates the ease with which Quin's mind separates the actual from the perceived, and helps the reader understand the importance to Quin of personal control. The event is partly metaphorical to ensure our experience of Quin's mind, but it is constantly controlled by the author's explanations. A more extended instance occurs when Barker becomes involved in Wayne's war, and all his perceptions become disoriented. The reader is allowed to experience the event through the rhythmic metaphors of Barker's story, but again only against careful authorial control which distances the emotions and fears expressed.

The technique is most clearly demonstrated at the moment when Quin finds his lunch interrupted by the first skirmish of the war. After building up a series of metaphors around the red uniform of Wayne's men, the narrator says:

> Then something happened which he was never able afterwards to describe, and which we cannot describe for him. (119)

After this disclaimer the author proceeds to describe. Wayne is then created as a vision of symbolic strength counterpointed against the grammatical control of the paragraphs and the uncertain note of Quin seeing him 'he knew not how'. But Quin and the reader are swept into an experience of Wayne as a symbol, and of his symbolic expression. But while the experience is necessary for both the character and reader because fundamental questions of self-expression are being evaluated, the danger of chaos inherent in the many interpretations possible from metaphor, is controlled by a careful use of explanation to ensure a defined comprehension. The relationship between Quin and Wayne is clarified by the experience and we feel with Quin that Wayne's communication is the more valuable. But the judgement is made with constant authorial guidance.

In many places, especially during the account of the war, the novelist's emphasis on explanation is too great. It slows the movement and dulls the response to the chapters. In contrast the final chapter of the novel is an earnest attempt to create experience without too much control; and it generates a feeling that defines and gives value to the story. The chapter begins in the darkness before sun-rise with two voices speaking, and the voices carry on a dialogue concerning the value of Notting Hill. As the night begins to lift, the men continue to give their opinions and explain their positions; and when the first silver of a new day becomes visible, the two humans are revealed as Wayne and Quin. The constant references to the growing light counterpoint the growing understanding between the two men as Quin reveals his joke and Wayne his acceptance of it. Their explanation of each other and of themselves concludes with Quin's statement that 'nothing can alter the antagonism – the fact that I laughed at these things and you adored them'. But Wayne's inspiration, that found its form for communication in Quin's joke, recognises the essential need for unity between the two men. The revelation comes to him simultaneously with the dawn; and in the now 'blank white light', Quin agrees. The two join together and go off to meet the world.

The explanation of the differing positions of Quin and Wayne is placed against the rising sun. The dawn is carefully integrated with each step in the growing knowledge of the two men, even though the metaphor is never allowed complete rein. In restricting the amount of explanation and closely integrating it with metaphor, Chesterton completely changes the tone of the chapter. No other part of the book stands out quite so sharply; no other part is so open to the reader's own involvement and interpretation. The reader not only sees the intellectual value of a balance between the conscious and unconscious control, but also experiences a personal value in it through the metaphor of the rising sun.

But it cannot be forgotten that Chesterton does not trust metaphor. He allows it to exist only in tandem with explanation, which however necessary to the meaning, curtails the potential experience. The fact that the style is heavily weighted towards emblem indicates the extent of the author's anxiety. Chesterton seems intuitively to acknowledge that perfect human expression, as proposed in the novel, is impossible in actual life. Small hints of another potential mode occur in the actions of an incidental character, the President of Nicaragua. He pins the yellow of a mustard advertisement to his shirt, and stabs his hand to provide the red colour of blood, yellow and red being his national colours. The action is not emblematic, it does not stand for anything. It is not metaphorical, for it does not recreate experience. It seems more directly connected to pure inspiration, yet is a definite, unmistakeable expression of patriotism. But the implications of his actions are not pursued.

Chesterton has tried to make a case for the balance between external and personal inspiration, to show the spontaneous inspiration receiving consciously controlled form. But he only succeeds in demonstrating that human expression is severely limited. In *G.F. Watts*, which was also written in 1904, the critic indicated a similar division between conscious and unconscious or spontaneous form. There he also implied that the unconscious divine inspiration alone communicated value. We have seen in the previous chapter that in *Heretics* Chesterton was beginning to think that opinions are only valuable when they indicate a conscious belief in an external. This idea, as well as the suggestion that ritual may be the best form for expressing the external, are both found in his next novel.

The Ball and the Cross was partially written in the same year as *Heretics*, and probably completed by 1906. In it Chesterton studies two men who both believe in something. One, Turnbull, has a reasonable basis for belief, centred finally in man and bounded by the limits of human understanding. The other, McIan, believes because of inspiration from an external divine source. Both are presented as necessary aspects of human belief but neither has an adequate form of expression to provide a unity between them. Turnbull is a journalist; he concentrates on the material facets of expression and is always in danger of losing the essence of the object. McIan uses symbol to communicate and is in danger of slipping too far from the actuality of the object. In either case imbalance results in communication centred in self. While they appear to be the same basic duo as that in *The Napoleon of Notting Hill* they are not. McIan is the externally inspired artist and Turnbull the personal dogmatist like Shaw. In *Heretics* it was the lack of Shaw's indication of external inspiration that made questionable his dogma; and this novel can be seen as an examination of the necessary fusion of the two aspects to gain precise communication. Further, there is a brief and not wholly successful study of a third character, Michael, and his mode of expression.

The style of *The Ball and the Cross* and the message about modes of communication, still run on different tracks. Here, however, the internal meaning does illuminate and, to an extent, confirms the author's form. There is a total explanatory control exerted over the complete work until the end of the book. The end provides neither explanation nor experience, but uses a different mode that only partially succeeds, and needs the content to be fully understood.

The conflict between the two main characters lies at the root of the meaning. It expresses itself most clearly in the dreams that the two men have when at the end of the book, they find themselves in an insane asylum. The atheist and individualist Turnbull is shown the result of discarding all external authority. The revolutionaries of his dream establish their freedom at the expense of other people's freedom. The ability of their minds to perceive limits collapses into a recognition of personal limits as the only definitions. In contrast McIan's dream shows authority taken to extremes and invalidating individual effort. In terms of perception, the external authority overwhelms the actual existence of the object, and sees only essence as important.

It is significant that both dreams occur in an asylum which harbours lunatics who believe themselves perfect. The denial of human limitation is the root of madness. The visions of Turnbull and McIan are their beliefs taken to extremes; they are thought of as perfect. And in both cases their modes of expression are revealed as inadequate. Yet while the novel gives the impression that there is a constant see-saw of discussion between McIan and Turnbull, which neither one wins, the argument is unbalanced; McIan is far more sympathetic. The basic parallels between the story and the framework equate McIan with the monk Michael and the cross, and Turnbull with Lucifer and the ball. Although Turnbull is a materialist, he does believe in actual identities; but this positive aspect is neglected. Further, the final revelation concerns the existence of an external authority. Initially Turnbull does not even believe in the external, let alone try to find a form to express it, so McIan has the edge from the start. The cross and the ball sum up the confusion. The central story of the novel attempts to show them in an equal balance with each other. Yet from the beginning the cross is more valuable, and at the end McIan says 'the great terrestrial globe will go quite lop-sided, and only the cross will stand upright'. The discrepancy not only results in a failure of the symmetrical structure of the novel, but also represents a serious confusion of ideas in Chesterton's thought. While supposedly admiring equally the opinions of the self and those of an absolute, he intuitively favours the latter.

The problem is compounded by the recognition that McIan's opinions although favoured are expressed in an demonstrably inadequate form. Chesterton felt that metaphor was too experiential to express absolute inspiration in *The Napoleon of Notting Hill*. The fear of didacticism and impressionism that result from the weakness led to a careful including of the explanatory in the experiential events. While McIan's symbolism is definitely shown to be the more powerful mode of expression, it is counteracted with an unwavering, conscious control by the author. No event of potential feeling or experience is expressed through metaphor which could potentially become arbitrary and impressionist. The main artistic technique used in the novel is emblem, and the function of emblem as 'standing for' something else, is painstakingly spelled out in the initial discussion between Michael and Lucifer about the meaning of the ball and the cross.

But just as McIan and Turnbull recognise their inadequacy when they reach the garden of human perfection and of madness, the novelist here too comes to terms with the inadequacy of his style. A mere balance between the two characters would leave open the potential dangers of each, but the monk Michael provides one answer for both. His miraculous walk through the flames of the burning asylum is a solid, acceptable fact to Turnbull even though it is not purely materialist; to McIan it is an actual representation of the power of God. Material and inspired expression fuse in this action. It is one form combining the two and delivering them from the dangers of balance.

The style of the final chapters is similar to that of Michael's walk through the flames. The garden and the asylum no longer stand for something, they are the actual. The dreams of Turnbull and McIan are unexplained but clear. They do not provide experience but indicate meaning alone. In the same way events surrounding their imprisonment are not explained. Intellectual reasons could be found for the details but they would not be adequate, and experiencing the imprisonment leaves the universal implications of the events enigmatic. The style, like Michael's walk, is an actual event; in other words not emblematic or symbolic. It contains rational meaning and indicates an experience. Yet the full expression implies more than these aspects; it points to a meaning that we cannot fully understand, but that we can know: the existence of an external and absolute authority.

The indication of essence is Chesterton's definition of the process of ritual. However in a novel it must be transformed into its verbal mode of allegory which aims to indicate with little or no interference by the author personally. But Michael is not a strong enough figure to carry the meaning. The author has constructed the novel as Michael's vision by beginning and ending the story with him. His character is established at the start. Although the reader recognises Michael in the conclusion, he is not sufficiently connected to a deeply-rooted meaning. The previously discussed confusion in Chesterton's use of the ball and the cross weakens Michael's effectiveness. The cross is the one external figure with which he is allied, and it loses its strength by being allied to the supposed balance between McIan and Turnbull that is shown to be an inevitable imbalance. Yet Michael's role in the story clarifies his function in the style. Although neither he, nor the form he presents, completely succeed, the character is important as an initial attempt at a mode that Chesterton will develop and refine to his own expressive needs as he matures.

ii

In the search for form Chesterton has examined nonsense, emblem, symbol and material description. Behind these modes exists a growing recognition of ritual in the actions of the President of Nicaragua and the monk Michael. In *The Ball and the Cross* Michael has a unique expression of ritual that brings together the actual and the essence. In 1906 the critic further defines his idea through the appreciation of folklore in *Charles Dickens*. The folklore is based on the ritualisation of aspects of people by exaggeration which transcends the separation of essence and form. The critic condemns the realism of the later novels although it is better art, because it tries to imitate where folklore does not. The control of folklore admits the limits of the artist because it indicates meaning beyond him; yet the control of realism implies a confidence in self that denies limits. Folklore is ritual and externally based; whereas realism is centred in the self and open to misinterpretation. These different criteria and the modes they generate become the central theme of Chesterton's next novel.

The Man Who Was Thursday was written in 1907, the year of an increasing confidence in the essays. There is a force to the book not felt in the earlier work. It is not a joke, nor a disputation, but a clear expression of Chesterton's inspiration. The novel explores many modes of expression and shows them all failing. At the end ritual takes over to justify and provide meaning for the events. All other modes communicate essence as far as the human can see it, but are ultimately inadequate. However, the author states that despite their brilliant technique, they are not 'better art', that any mode leading to potential anarchy and despotism is not only immoral but also inartistic. The novelist finally differentiates between morality and ethics. He refuses to accept that the artist can avoid moral responsibility and depend on a self-centred code of conduct.

The artist now has two essential roles: those of artist and critic that Chesterton looked at in *Charles Dickens* when comparing himself to the novelist. He must function critically in perceiving the essence of the thing, and creatively in expressing that essence. The division must not be confused with that between the impressionist and inspirational, or didactic and dogmatic separations of the earlier novels. The two roles are not antagonistic, in conflict or in balance. They are both part of the same process in one man. The emphasis of the book is on both interpretation and representation of essence by the artist; and is far more mature in its recognition of the complexity of the issues. The dual role of the artist seems to put Chesterton at ease. It necessitates admission of human limitation, yet allows for creation. The conclusion of both the content and the style is that ritual is the only form which satisfies both conditions, and that allegory is the artistic mode that expresses ritual.

The novel begins in a London suburb. The resident poet Gregory, presents himself as an anarchist, and is in the middle of holding forth when a poet of order, Gabriel Syme, turns up. After an argument, Gregory takes Syme with him to a meeting of the English anarchists who are just about to elect him to their European Council. Syme first has to promise not to reveal anything to the police. Then he in turn makes Gregory promise not to reveal him to the anarchists, for he is a police detective. Putting this mutual secrecy to use Syme gets himself elected to the Council instead of Gregory. He becomes Thursday, the day of the week allotted to the English member. The European Council meets the next day under their president, Sunday. After the unexpected exposure of Tuesday as a policeman, the remaining anarchists plot the death of the czar who is visiting France, and then break up. Throughout the central section of the novel Syme is involved in tracking down the individual members of the Council to try to halt the plot. One by one they are revealed as police detectives.

First he meets Friday, Professor Worms; together they expose Saturday, Dr Bull, and all leave for France. When they reveal Wednesday or Ratcliffe, they find that Monday, the one remaining anarchist has got an army together to destroy them. They escape to the edge of the sea where Monday tries to arrest them in the name of the law, for he too is a policeman. Confused but relieved they return to England to find out who Sunday is. There is an absurd chase through London and the countryside which leads them to Sunday's house where they are looked after and feasted. The book ends with them asking why it all happened. Then Sunday disappears and Syme wakes up to find himself walking along a road talking to Gregory.

Sunday is the key to the meaning of Syme's experience. He is also the guide to the overall meaning of the book. Sunday is introduced first as the leader of the anarchists: a powerful, intelligent man, commanding respect. It should be noted that at the beginning of the central section a similar figure is introduced as the head of the police force. He is unseen, always living in a dark room. Sunday, by contrast, is almost 'too large to see'. As Syme approaches him he is overcome by a sense of 'spiritual evil' that grows with the face of Sunday. The sense gets stronger, and Syme is afraid that the face will grow so large it will be impossible to see, and he is reminded of seeing the face of Memnon as a child at the Britism Museum. Sunday's position as an anarchist is weakened in the central section of the novel when he himself begins the break-up of the Council by exposing Tuesday. When all the policemen are revealed, the third action begins and the reader meets Sunday once more. Syme asks him who he is. His only answer is that they can never know, only that he was also the policeman in the dark room. Each member tries to define him in his own terms, and each relates him in a different way to life. Sunday is seen as the two sides of man, the animal and the god. Finally he becomes a fusion of the two initial images of the seen and the unseen men:

> the great face grew to an awful size, grew larger than the colossal mask of Memnon, which had made him scream as a child. It grew larger and larger, filling the whole sky; then everything went black. (191)

The answer to who he is lies in his last words, 'Can ye drink of the cup that I drink of?' It is both enigmatic yet satisfying.

The shifting definition of Sunday parallels Syme's state of mind. In the first section of three chapters he is sure that he is a poet of the law. He knows the difference between anarchy and order; between Sunday and the man in the dark room. Sunday, however, begins the process that exposes the policemen, exposes order. Paradoxically, Syme, in continuing these exposures, becomes an anarchist. At the moment of becoming an anarchist he is revealed as a policeman. Throughout the central section he attempts to make sense of the situation, and when all the men are exposed it seems that the meaning of things should be clear, but it is not. Without Sunday being defined, none of the members can be properly defined. The dual role of Sunday which the final three chapters slowly clarifies, helps Syme understand why he had to become an anarchist. At the end he realises that he will never completely understand Sunday or himself; but he can know of Sunday's existence and that it justifies his own.

Sunday's definition also parallels the style of the novel. The first section is filled with explanation on both the author's and the poet's part. There are many carefully placed images with isolated and detached significance. The whole is constructed to set up the opposing sides of order and anarchy, and the rigid division reinforces the definiteness of Syme's attitude to law, and Sunday's initial duality. In common with the confusion of the central section, the style transposes impressionism and clarity within each exposure of the policeman. The final section is written as an allegory, allowing the characters to participate in ritual which eludes understanding but points to one external authority. The author's confidence, or perhaps trust, in his new mode helps him for once to create an integrated work. The message of his story and the function of his style are very close to each other. Syme and the writer go through the same process of expression with the progress of events, and the events themselves illuminate the meaning of the expression.

The action of the novel begins with the establishing of roles for the poet of order and the poet of anarchy. Paradoxically we find that the anarchist has to be far more organised to survive as such than the poet of order; and he is introduced while speaking in 'his high didactic voice, laying down the law'. Syme, on the other hand, is engaged by the police force as a free agent with no questions asked. Despite his passionate defence of respectability he is a 'meek' and 'humble' man. But the novelist provides a more important comment on the two men in his opening style. Both men are shown as definite; both use similar emblematic examples, merely interpreted from their own point of view. Their claim to full understanding makes both poets over-explain in these first three chapters. The author allows it and the action of the chapters is arrested by the very limitations that are being exposed in the characters. Neither man has a satisfactory outlook; neither the control nor the spontaneity they represent can succeed in isolation.

Within this first section a second point of stylistic importance originates. The novelist establishes certain random, rather fanciful images concerning red hair which is associated negatively with Gregory and positively with his sister. There is also a musical motif in the barrel-organ which inspires Syme. The associative and am-biguous nature of these images is appropriate to the artistic limitations of author and characters which appear in this section of the novel. As these limitations are broken down and explored, the images will come to form an integral part of the personal symbolic expression that results from a less isolated view of communication.

Syme's intended role within the police force emerges from a conversation with another policeman at the start of the central section. There is apparently a 'purely intellectual conspiracy' threatening the existence of civilisation. The police are expected to 'trace the origin of these dreadful thoughts that drive men on at last to intellectual fanaticism and intellectual crime'. These are the thoughts that 'stop thought'; Gregory himself says that the anarchists want 'To abolish God', to make themselves the sole source of meaning for the world. This of course is Chesterton's solipsistic vision. Yet here he says that total despotic control to counteract it is just as bad. Syme must find another solution to come to terms with the 'dreadful thoughts'.

The growth into anarchy by the characters in the central section of the novel, is paralleled by a growth of more and more impressionism in expression. The process begins when Syme accepts the role of Thursday and steps into the steamship that will take him to his meeting with the Council. The transition from order to anarchy is stylistically one from explanation to impressionism, and the novelist carefully combines the two aspects at the end of the first section. But both the impression and explanation are transcended by the actual objects Syme carries with him: his food, brandy and pistol. They take on a 'concrete and material poetry' which conveys his true inspiration. Syme can reach beyond impression to inspiration, and it is the growth of his ability to do so that we watch as he experiences and comes terms with anarchy.

Significantly the first anarchist council member that Syme meets is the Secretary, or Monday, the pure intellectual at the root of the conspiracy. The other men on the council each represent different uses of intellect for the perversion of logic. Syme thinks on seeing them that:

> Each figure seemed to be, somehow, on the borderland of things, just as their theory was on the borderline of thought. He knew that each one of these men stood at the extreme end, so to speak, of some wild road of reasoning. (64)

The members of the Council are all aspects of man; and Syme as the poet or definer has to discover the meaning that lies beyond their appearance. The only clue comes from Sunday when he exposes Tuesday. Tuesday stands out as the obvious choice, the madman, the fanatic; but the whole man is a pose. The Russian peasant is a harmless Cockney business man with a little blue card that identifies him as a policeman.

But it is the inspirational artist in Syme that initially proves most valuable in discovering the anarchists' identities. The initial mask of each man is established during the first meeting, and Syme describes them as 'demonic details' that he tries to shake off, but 'The sense of an unnatural symbolism always settled back on him again'. The feeling marks a process of apprehension that does not right itself until each figure is exposed. Syme counteracts the fear caused by separation of essence and form, when he hears the jangle of a barrel-organ. It suddenly recalls to him his source of true inspiration: the Church, the 'common and kindly people in the street', his humanity. As he listens, the image of the barrel-organ that the reader was briefly introduced to in section one is enriched. It becomes a metaphor, rooted in the actual and conveying the real. Through it Syme controls the fear of the vague impressions around him and pierces to their inspiration.

The first exposure in which he is directly involved is that of Professor Worms. Here Syme only instigates the exposure because the Professor reveals himself by producing his little blue card, and only then does Syme produce his. The Professor's facade was as a propounder of German nihilism. On dropping his mask he reveals a realist. Realism stands at the beginning of a self-dependence that leads in the end to a denial of all authority. This is why his anarchic form is nihilism. When Syme is in the process of discovering the true inspiration his own impressions are distorted in a nihilistic manner. After a few attempts to escape the Professor who follows him after the meeting, he feels that the 'philosophical entities called time and space have no vestige even of practical existence'. Against this vague indefiniteness, the distortion of nihilistic perception, Syme suddenly notices, picked 'out in perfect silver, the great orb and cross'. He counteracts the effects of the totally arbitrary images with the 'symbol of human faith and valour' and gains the courage to turn and face his pursuer. When the Professor is exposed, Syme:

> had for a flash the sensation that the cosmos had turned exactly upside down, . . . Then came slowly the opposite conviction. For the last twenty-four hours the cosmos had really been upside

down, but now the capsized universe had come right side up again.
(85)

The peculiar effect of the professor's perverted realism was conquered
by the use of symbol which never claims total personal control; and
which expresses the essence of the order for which Syme is fighting.

In a similar manner Syme goes on to expose Bull's rationalism and
efficiency as an ordinary practicality by means of inspiration from his
personal symbol of a woman's red hair. The same symbol, along with
the barrel-organ, instigates his exposure of the fourth member,
Wednesday or Radcliffe. His aestheticism and cynicism is the result of
the reduction of common sense by the intellectual perversion of
anarchy. The common sense of Radcliffe lets him naturally take
charge of the band of policemen as they retreat from the army which
is led by Monday. In the flight from the perverted logic of pure
intellect Syme is overcome by the most dangerous impressionism of
all, the doubt of his own existence. The shadows of the wood into
which they retreat cause confusion, and the disorientation increases
until Syme wonders:

> was he wearing a mask? Was anyone wearing a mask? Was anyone
> anything . . . Was there anything apart from what it seemed? . . .
> He had found . . . that final scepticism which can find no floor to
> the universe. (133)

The poet pulls himself out of this doubt by sheer conversation; and it
is dispelled by the appearance of a peasant cutting wood, who was
'common-sense in an almost awful actuality'. Yet the confusion of
identity experienced recurs as one by one the men the police think
they can rely on, turn about face and help the anarchists.

From Syme's perspective Monday is the last remaining anarchist.
He is the intellect that provides the basis of anarchy. Yet from
Monday's own perspective, he is the last remaining policeman for he
is philosophy that stops anarchy. The progress of Syme has
increasingly isolated him from the rest of the world as he has defined
the personal basis of the members' lives. Near the end of the chase
Syme warns the Professor that he's becoming an anarchist, and
Radcliffe adds 'Everyone is'. Syme has become an anarchist even
though he thinks he is still a policeman. The paradox arises from the
realisation that the personal meaning he has uncovered has no
absolute basis. Once the personal inspiration for the men's behaviour

is clarified by Syme's poetic creation, it does not seem to help to define their lives. To avoid anarchy Syme must define with reference to an external authority which means interpretation as well as creation, and this he has increasingly ceased to do.

With every normal expectation reversed, on the edge of giving in to the insanity of the solipsist, Syme's personal symbols of the red hair and the barrel-organ are now useless as a means to inspire him. He turns to a different mode of expression to counteract the impressionism of the intellect. At the last minute he picks up the old ecclesiastic lamp a helper had given him, and challenges Monday. By the allegorical meaning of 'the cross carved on it, and the flame inside', he tears away the intellectual scepticism of Monday to expose him as a policeman; in the process he also exposes himself. Allegory is externally inspired rather than personally created alone. It cannot, therefore, degenerate into impressionism or rationalism, and includes its own interpretation. This final exposure casts off human intellect to reveal external authority for action; it casts off human expression to acknowledge that it is too limited to define man. The simultaneous exposure of Monday and Syme as both policeman and anarchist is the recognition of control and spontaneity as two essential elements in man. Further it is the recognition that they cannot simultaneously exist without the acknowledgement of an external authority and inspiration; and that this authority cannot be expressed through human symbol, but only through ritual in allegory.

The creative nature of Syme's exposure in the central section of the book was necessary for him to understand his human limitations. In the final section his role as poet or definer is mainly interpretive in the light of these limitations. The last section shows the men trying to define Sunday because they realise that their personal meaning is not complete without him. Yet it is not until they become involved in the ritual he has created for them that they succeed, and Syme leads the way in the attempt. It is he who starts the totally absurd chase into the countryside.

The limits of man's understanding are underlined as each man tries to define Sunday while on the chase. Each definition is an aspect of man that is not understood. For example, Monday thinks of him as like 'protoplasm . . . the final form of matter', which reminds him of all that human intellect originated in, and over which it has virtually no power. Syme begins to notice and interpret the pattern that defines Sunday only by negatives. Relating the pattern of negative definitions to his own experience, he reaches the 'secret of the whole world', that man always looks only at the back of things, never at the front. Syme realises that he has been exposing the back of people, the human nature. His great revelation is that he must search for the face, the god-like, the divine.

The revelation ends the chase, yet would not have been possible if the men had not been involved in it. The chase can be seen as performing different functions for every expressive level. As an action involving the council it is a ritual they must perform in order to understand Sunday. For Sunday it is an allegorical expression of the ritual. For Chesterton both allegory and ritual are themselves an allegorical expression of life. Rather than an absurdity without logic, it is an enigma with an unknown logic; and enigma is the central feature of Chesterton's allegory. Apart from the chase itself one of the enigmatic aspects is the dropping of notes for each man. The notes indicate on a smaller scale the function of allegory. They contain some application to the recipient, but every reader will get something different from them. For example, Syme's note reads:

No one would regret anything in the nature of an interference by the Archdeacon more than I. I trust it will not come to that. But, for the last time, where are your goloshes? The thing is too bad, especially after what uncle said. (164)

One response is to see the contrast between Syme's occasionally ludicrous sense of form and ceremony and his neglect of practicalities. A simpler example is found in the note to Tuesday. As the supposed anarchist Russian peasant, or 'red', his note reads, 'The word, I fancy, should be "pink"'. What is important is that the notes have some relevance for each person, but one can never understand them fully. A more important enigmatic and allegorical aspect is the use of clothes. The chase ends when a messenger arrives from Sunday to take the men to his house. Here the members are all given clothes which define them. This time their definition is not personal but absolute for Sunday's allegory does 'not disguise, but reveal'.

At the final ceremony all the animals and objects that have been encountered in the book are dancing at what seems a pointless masquerade until Sunday appears and then the dancing becomes 'as absurd as Alice in Wonderland, yet as grave and kind as a love story'. The confluence of nonsense and romance in the ritual dance indicates Chesterton's understanding of allegory as without comprehensible logic yet with an absolute goal and authority. However, the appearance of Sunday leads the men to question why the Anarchic Council was set up; why they should have suffered. Again each question is appropriate to the aspect of human nature each member represents.

As they finish questioning, Gregory, the true anarchist poet, reappears. It is after his accusation that the policemen are mere acceptors of law, never having truly suffered, that Syme makes his last definition, his final interpretation of the action of the book. The men had to become anarchists, to suffer, to define themselves, before their function within and understanding of an external system of order could become valuable. But when he questions Sunday, because it is important for his own value to know that Sunday too should have suffered, he is answered with the words 'Can ye drink of the cup that I drink of?' and Syme blacks out before the impossible knowing of God. Simultaneous with Gregory's appearance is the reintroduction of Syme's personal symbols of the 'red hair'. One again has the duality of Gregory's red hair which 'shall burn up the world' and the opposite force of his having 'red hair like your sister'. Yet just as the ambiguity and danger of authority and anarchy in man is explained, so the ambiguity and danger of the personal symbol is here resolved in face of an external authority. When Syme comes to it, it is as if his participation in ritual has strengthened his personal expression. Having defined himself in terms of an external he can use symbol with new clarity, and the novel ends with the 'gold-red hair' of Gregory's sister.

The novel as a whole does contain an overriding control by Chesterton. However, the control is constructed as ritual so that a lot depends upon the connections the reader makes with a meaning beyond the story itself. As with the previous novels, *The Man Who Was Thursday* takes place at twilight, the time of change. It is also enclosed, this time by a dream framework which is significant when one remembers that Chesterton believed dreams to present essence despite seemingly inappropriate exteriors. The movement is circular in beginning with Syme and Gregory at the start, returning to them in the last chapter. Yet here the movement does not lead to some projected human perfection of expression. It returns to the limited symbolic mode of man, showing it stabilised by participation in ritual. The parallels between the events and the style show that personal definition through understanding is linked with the human process of impression and inspiration. The ethical foundation of this understanding is not adequate to prevent the danger of anarchy or despotism. Instead definition must be approached through the knowledge of an external authority that is experienced in, and interpreted from, the allegorical verbalisation of ritual. The basis of existence will then be absolute and moral.

It is important that within the novel the ritual is given by the Christian God. Therefore the characters of the book can find it perfectly revealing. Because it is written by Chesterton the ritual cannot be perfect in the reader's terms. It is humanly limited and intended to be so. The formal and obvious structuring of the book into three sections, the allegorical rather than symbolic function of the characters, and the absurdity of temporal and spatial relations, make this clear. Yet Chesterton has chosen a sufficiently strong allegory to present the meaning, in using the days of the week and their biblical interpretations. The weight of such figures transcends the limitations of the human expression, just as the ecclesiastical lamp transcended the ultimate danger of limited human understanding. Chesterton's confidence lies in this knowledge of having incorporated an external authority. Yet the novel also contains a symbolic strength that is new to Chesterton's novels and makes it possible for the reader not just to observe but to involve himself in the work. In his own terms he has both perceived essence in an acknowledgedly limited way, yet expressed it creatively and with moral responsibility as an artist.

6 Developing the Land: 1908—1912

Both Chesterton's artistic and critical writing takes on a new maturity and confidence in tone during the year 1907, and it cannot be forgotten that also during 1907 he was writing the statement of his acceptance of the Anglo-Catholic church: *Orthodoxy*. Not surprisingly the book was written in answer to a reviewer of *Heretics*, G. S. Street, who challenged Chesterton to state an alternative dogma. In *Orthodoxy* Chesterton not only provides the first consistent background to his religious and philosophical beliefs, but also states the primary aspects of his mature concept of art. Until writing *Orthodoxy* Chesterton has, in his critical work, concentrated on a negative view of religion and art: what they should not be, rather than what they should be. Just as *The Man Who Was Thursday* exuded a new-found confidence because of his discovery of a satisfactory form, in this book we find at the root of all the ideas a positive recognition of a specific external authority. To satisfy the principles of his belief, Chesterton found that the authority had to be the Christian God within formal religion.

At the end of Chapter Four in *Orthodoxy* Chesterton outlines the five principles of his belief. The first is that since the world does not explain itself it needs a miracle to do so. The next follows logically: there must be someone to work this miracle necessarily external to the world. The third states that the purpose of the world is beautiful; and fourth, that man must have gratitude for the purpose by showing humility and restraint. Finally, the existence of 'good' is a positive gift to man, and a thing to be saved. The only authority to satisfy all these beliefs for Chesterton was the Christian God. Christianity had half led him to, and half reinforced his belief in, certain dominant ideas. Because there is an external authority the experience of revelation becomes possible. Since man cannot know himself by human means, identity is something that is revealed to him. This emphasises the difference in kind rather than degree between man and God; man is both human and divine. It also makes possible a divine transcendence of the separation between essence and matter. We have seen all these ideas explored in *The Man Who Was Thursday*, and they have a direct bearing on the writer's changing concept of art.

Orthodoxy was written to state that Christian theology provided the most sound basis for life. Chesterton included not only the celebration of life which he found in it, but also the fear from which it guarded him. The book turns the treatment of art in *The Man Who Was Thursday* into a philosophical discussion on the nature of man, and it reaches a more clearly defined but identical conclusion. He begins with a study of the 'madman', specifically the solipsistic kind who believes that he is the creator of, and at the centre of, the world. Formal religious authority is found necessary to stop this 'thought that stops thought': the absurdity of the situation man is reduced to when he is left with only himself to explain the world. The willingness he shows actually to speak about the existence of the fear is significant. The earlier avoidance of the underlying knowledge that it was present, was directly responsible for the negative approach to art and religion that he had previously taken. Chesterton had been seeking to repress, rather than find a positive antidote or cure.

Here, however, the celebration of life is his central concern, and it is summed up for him in the allegory of the cross:

> the cross, though it has at its heart a collision and a contradiction, can extend its four arms for ever without altering its shape. Because it has a paradox at its centre it can grow without changing. (29)

The doctrine of the church was intended to keep 'seemingly inconsistent' things side by side. Virtue itself was a conflict between two ideas 'hard to hold simultaneously'. Not only are love and wrath, joy and sorrow, kept together; but so also are the divine and animal of man, the essence and substance of things, and the idea and mode of expression. The external authority of God makes possible a transcendence of the division; it makes possible transcendence of human limitations.

Chesterton finds his positive joy in the formal, defined structure of the Anglo-Catholic church. An acceptance of the external authority of God meant that things existed outside himself; actual things were real. It also meant that man did not create *ex nihilo*. He used the pre-existing material of each artistic language to express essence. Further, the existence of God makes possible a belief in ritual as a valuable mode of expression, for without God the built-in limitations of ritual itself could be distorted. We have seen that in his own art he at first emphasised the role of control in order to conquer the changes of impressionism, and that this went against the grain when it became despotic. It weakened the structure of his books by producing a conflict between the stylistic and thematic meaning. The acceptance of external formal religion led to an expression of ritual through allegory that resolved this conflict. Similarly, the insistence on control in other people's opinions weakened the strength of Chesterton's criticism, because he often disagreed with the personal opinion while believing that opinion itself should be there. Once he accepted external authority he had a positive basis for his criticism, and he could suggest the use of the analogy of ritual in forms of fairy-tale, anecdote or allegory.

Much of the critical confusion that was caused by transforming the interrelationship between inspiration, art and life into one between religion, morality, and expression had been clarified by 1907. It arose from the problem of differentiating between personal and external authority, between ethics and morality and between the artist as solely creator and the artist as creator and interpreter. *Orthodoxy* shows that the differentiation has essentially been made. Chesterton discusses the moral function of man as necessarily found in an exercise of will. But the term 'will' is used to mean divine revelation in man. It also connects the religious belief with artistic expression. One exercises will not rationally, but 'like an artist, saying, "I *feel* this curve is right"'. This does not imply a vague process of selection; it is an acknowledgement of an external authority that constantly reminds man of his limitations, and the author goes on to define art as limitation. The whole basis for his stated attitude to religion and art is found in the analogy he uses to indicate the presence of God:

> God was a creator, as an artist is a creator. A poet is so separate from his poem that he himself speaks of it as a little thing he has 'thrown off'. (78)

The positive value in Christianity is 'the dogmatic insistence that God was personal, and had made a world separate from himself'. Just as he accepts that God is different in kind from man, so is the artist different from his art, because he cannot create the absolute reality that is himself. If man needs God to reveal his identity, then matter needs the artist to give it meaning. Just as a man is not the centre of the world, so art does not exist in isolation. Man must be constantly aware of his human limitations to remain sane, and art must acknowledge limitations of its own.

What is here developing is Chesterton's concept of the mystic artist. The separated nature of the artist and the art is conveyed most fully in the function of the mystic which lies at the core of his new positive attitude. The mystic not only indicates the separation between matter and essence, but also acknowledges the separation between his mode of expression and the object. The mystic can accept his limitation. If a man does not, he is either damned or mad; he either makes a conscious, or an unconscious, wrong, moral choice. So, the author says that, 'Mysticism keeps man sane' because it allows one to separate earth and fairy land, whereas ordinary men live in the twilight between the two. He defines the twilight images of the earlier novels as a compromise undermining the conflict that he now finds necessary. An early article on the mysticism of W. B. Yeats said, 'true Mysticism will have nothing to do with twilight'; and in another essay: 'Actuality is the keynote of Mysticism'.[1] The function of the mystic is to recognise not only his separation from his art, but also the separation between matter and essence. The separations that the mystic indicates are valuable because they represent a relationship that reveals the presence of God as the power which transcends their differences. The role of the mystic is to perceive this relationship and communicate it so that others too can realise the existence of the divine.

That the mystic communicates is in Chesterton's eyes absolutely essential. It is partly the author's own conversion from personal to formal religion that makes him emphasise the social function of communication. Without the communication of the relationship the mystic perceives, there will be not only no valuable assertion given to society as a whole, but also no conception of the human limitation of the mystic. The limiting process of expression ensures that the mystic does not exercise too personal a control; if he does, the presence of the divine, which the relationship reveals, may be lost sight of. Only in accepting the limits of expression does it become possible to transcend the division between the mode and idea, to find identity of oneself and the object. The mystic maintains his artistic responsibility by insisting on the actual existence of the object in which he can only indicate, not create, divine presence. If he does not do this, he will impose his personal perception on things; he will distort their meaning by making them become part of himself rather than letting them remain separate. This was the definition given earlier to the degenerate fantasist, the failing Dickens.

In his idea of the mystic Chesterton is significantly different from ideas in the serious study of mysticism being carried out at this time, probably because his philosophy was maturing in a very personal manner. At no point did Chesterton set out to establish a doctrine for himself, ready-made and complete. His ideas slipped into place one by one, continually shifting and re-arranging themselves. He never belonged to a school and as a result was often contributing ideas antagonistic to current streams of thought. Yet he had the advantage of being able to see farther and in many cases with more originality than his contemporaries. The main theory of mysticism at this time was that it was intellectual or spiritual. William James, for example, says that 'personal religious experience has its root and centre in mystical states of consciousness', and believes that mystical experience is totally incommunicable to other people. Dean Inge, who led the Christian mystic movement, saw it as completely intellectual, 'Christian Mysticism appears in history largely as an intellectual movement, the foster-child of Platonic idealism'. In his view the mystic 'makes it his life's aim to be transformed into the likeness of Him in whose image he was created'. The experience is also thought to be too spiritual for normal utterance; and therefore without social value. Inge's views on religion were both anti-rationalist and anti-formalist, and in philosophy, anti-sceptical and anti-material. Chesterton, of course, insists on the material and actual aspect of the mystic vision; he also insists on its communicability and its social value. We can recognise here that his later annoyance with Dean Inge rested largely on the Dean's belief that Roman Catholicism, because it was institutional, was also anti-mystical.

However, Chesterton's idea is virtually identical with that of Evelyn Underhill, who expresses the attitude clearly 13 years later in *The Essentials of Mysticism*. Underhill conjectures the existence of three stages in mysticism: the physical, the mental and the spiritual. Yet if one progresses up to the spiritual, it is always essential to return to the value of the physical. Similarly, although the mystic 'appears to be independent of the general religious consciousness of the community', he needs both society and the Church for his own physical unity. If their physical existence is not in tune with his, he will be constantly in conflict between spirit and matter. It will also become difficult 'for him to avoid the disease of spiritual megalomania' which is exactly Chesterton's point about the dangers of the solipsistic view raising its head if there is no social contact. Underhill notes the positive side as well. The mystic experience revitalises the Church if it is communicated, and the mystic is 'a creative personality, consecrated to the great practical business of actualizing the eternal order in the temporal'. Because he must mediate he is the highest form of creative artist; he must see things as they really are without personal distortion. Underhill also realises that in mystical literature the words must not be confused with the things. They express, but are not, the truth.

In *Orthodoxy* Chesterton is very much concerned with the problem of expression. Symbols are condemned as of 'cloudy value' when speaking of the infinite. Metaphor is useless unless it can convey a 'distinct' idea. Finally he laments his own 'unavoidable inadequacy, the attempt to utter unutterable things'. A later essay expresses his feelings this way:

> there is something in all good things that is beyond all speech or figure of speech. But it is also true that there is in all good things a perpetual desire for expression and concrete embodiment . . .[2]

The mystic, therefore, has the problem of imaginatively creating a form that will communicate the separation between matter and essence. The forms Chesterton discusses at this time are the fairy-tale, the fable, song, dance and mumming. In each case the artist makes no attempt to create reality. Fairy-tale sets reasonable limits, distinguishes between real laws of mental choice and mere physical repetitions, and depends on specific conditions. Fables use animals because man is 'something too mysterious to be drawn'. Mumming conceals the personality but reveals the person.

Each form does not pretend to be the object but to indicate it by analogy, and the analogical function is the basis for all these forms. Analogy represents not only similarities but differences. The two things, image and object, lying side by side, transcend each other because of the divine relation between them. It is important to see the relation of analogy to nonsense. Nonsense logic also places two things side by side. But it either insists on an intellectual, man-generated relation between the two, or denies that any relation exists. The analogical function separates the artist from his art by denying him complete creativity. Yet it allows him to communicate the separation of matter and essence, and both limitations are transcended by the indication of the presence of the divine. Chesterton sees ritual as the fundamental analogy that relates man to God. As we have seen his own main verbal mode of expressing the analogy of ritual is allegory. While he later develops a more sophisticated view of allegory, *The Man Who Was Thursday* contains the basic elements of concrete imagery, gesture and allusion in the enigmatic use of the notes, the necessary action of the chase and the absolute definition of the robes Sunday gives to the council.

Most people writing about mysticism at the turn of the century express the same discontent about the mode of communicating mystic experience, just as the social anthropologists of the late nineteenth century were dissatisfied with the communication of religious ideas as a social manifestation. The relationship between ritual and mysticism in Chesterton's work is closely connected to early anthropological ideas about ritual and religion. He sits in a central position between the personal religions of Inge and James and the social religions of Frazer, Spenser and Durkheim. Yet it is interesting that none of these people really explored in depth the fundamental problem of the communication of religious and mystical experience.

Inge himself agrees with James that mystical experience cannot be conceptualised, that language is poor, inadequate and misleading. Normally substance and symbol have an accidental connection, but in mysticism the connection becomes real. The observation is reminiscent of the note of both Spenser and Frazer, that savages could not separate between object and symbol. Inge goes on to say that the closest one can get to the fusion of the two is in sacrament. The need for sacrament 'rests ultimately on the instinctive reluctance to allow any spiritual fact to remain without an external expression'. While this is similar to Chesterton's own earlier statement about an object's desire for expression, Inge denies the experience of transubstantiation, and the idea of allegory which says that 'The world was supposed to be full of sacred cryptograms'. His view of sacrament lacks the material and actual element that Chesterton is trying to incorporate, and he is therefore not faced with nearly as many expressive problems.

Emile Durkheim is far more thorough in trying to assess the forms of religious expression. But he begins his study with a quotation from Max Muller's *Physical Religion* which states that language and thought are of a different structure. Religious expression thus becomes a 'deformation' of language by belief. Later he goes on to say that emblems are of fundamental importance in overcoming this deformity. Flags, for example, lose their representative function in battle and are treated as if they 'were this reality [of the country] itself'. In religion images are not illusions, 'they correspond to something in reality' that connects the individual with society. Religious force, albeit social, 'comes to be outside of the object in which it resides' and is capable of transcending it. Further, Durkheim believes that social life is only possible with a vast system of emblems. It is not surprising that the first major mode Chesterton chooses is emblem. But whereas he comes to see this as potentially distortable, Durkheim does not interest himself in the actual manipulation of communication.

It is the 1920s that produces more sophisticated studies of the modes of religious and mystical expression. When we turn to them, however, we find they are remarkably close to the ideas of Chesterton in 1908. Rudolph Otto's *The Idea of the Holy* begins with the familiar statement that the holy completely eludes apprehension by concepts and is inexpressible. Yet he devotes much of his book to possible ways of communicating it. He says that if the divine is to be expressed verbally it must be through negatives and analogies which 'profess to indicate *an* object, which they at the same time contrast with another, at once distinct from and inferior to it'. Otto also examines what he calls a process of 'schematization' where associative images become one with the idea. Interestingly enough he parallels this with romantic 'sublimity', and indeed it is a close analysis of the function of symbol, the staple diet of Romantic literature. Finally he says that pure but indirect expression is given through fear and grandeur, and pure and direct expression in darkness and silence. Analogy is impure and functions by 'anamnesis' or a reminding of the divine. However Otto is concerned to preserve the irrational; to deepen rational Christianity with irrational thoughts. Chesterton is exactly the opposite. Where Otto finds irregularity in mystery and paradox, Chesterton finds order.

Evelyn Underhill again comes closest to Chesterton saying that the mystic has to use art to actualise the spiritual. Underhill proposes that there are two main ways in which this is effected: by description which appeals to the intellect, and suggestion which appeals to the imagination. In the process of examining each, many concepts found in Chesterton's criticism emerge. The descriptive writer tries to 'represent in concrete symbols the objective reality known'. He is 'naturally inclined to virtualization'. By contrast the allusive writer tries to represent the 'subjective feeling-state induced', using 'negative language' and paradox. Underhill finds the allusive artist more successful in 'putting us in communion with reality' than the descriptive artist, yet the latter 'is more generally understood'. Chesterton's later work uses both kinds of communication and tries to achieve both effects.

Of course Chesterton is not only a religious man, but also an artist and critic primarily interested in the function of words, much more so than the average theologian, mystic or anthropologist. Having seen the tools that were available to him in contemporary discussions on religious expression, it is useful to look at the relevance of his ideas to contemporary currents in literature and art. There are two movements which gather force at the close of the first decade of the century which are especially important: Imagism and surrealism. In their rejection of the predominantly symbolic and discursive modes of contemporary art, both are close to Chesterton's exploration for an alternative. On the one hand, having rejected as too dangerous for himself the potentially absolute human creativity of symbol, Chesterton could have aligned himself with the similar fears of the Imagist movement. On the other hand, he also rejected the distorting power of rationalism, and in his efforts to uncover another more reasonable logic, might later have found himself in the surrealist camp. Ideological differences kept him away from both, yet those differences themselves indicate the difficulty of what he was trying to do.

Imagism as a movement was much influenced by the thought of T. E. Hulme, and if we begin with Hulme's own ideas about the relationship of religion and art, we find that they are superficially identical to Chesterton's. 'Humanism and the Religious Attitude' is based on a study of the Renaissance as an age without religious art because of the predominance of humanist emotion. Hulme denies the value of imitative art and says the absolute ideas need absolute expression. In other essays he points out that since the Renaissance, philosophy has seen man at the centre of the world, and this is incorrect. 'Romanticism and Classicism' postulates that the Romantics took man as god, with rationalism as the supreme logical power. Against this he places classicism which never 'forgets this finiteness, this limit of man'.

There are many similarities between Hulme's and Chesterton's approach to art. They both insist on the need to see things as they really are; and to express them accurately, without the conventions of contemporary romantic art. Hulme says that:

In prose as in algebra concrete things are embodied in signs or

counters which are moved about according to rules . . .
Poetry . . . may be considered as an effort to avoid this . . . It is
not a counter language, but a visual concrete one. [3]

Hulme too emphasises the need for limitation in art. He speaks of the
need to impose order on impressionism, and of the futility of rational
argument even using the same vocabulary as Chesterton. However,
the fundamental differences in the application are huge. Hulme
opposes to the idea of 'man as god' the Hindu concept of the futility of
man. As an example of his ideal of modern religious expression he
puts forward Epstein's sculptures. It is interesting that Chesterton, in
1929 writes an essay 'On Mr. Epstein'. [4] In it he fully recognises the
religious content of the sculptures, but goes on to say that it is the
wrong religion. It is also ironic that the very words Hulme uses to
define his religion are echoed again and again by Chesterton when
indicating the wrong religion. For Hulme, man must avoid thinking
all things in his power by returning to the centres of external
inspiration; 'the result is that which follows the snake eating its own
tail, an *infinite* straight line *perpendicular* to the plane'. The basis for his
religion is 'most conveniently remembered by the symbol of the
wheel'. Compare this with Chesterton's comment in a story from *The
Incredulity of Father Brown*:

> I've scarcely ever met a criminal who philosophized at all, who
> didn't philosophize along those lines of orientalism and recurrence
> and reincarnation, and the wheel of destiny and the serpent biting
> his own tail. (144)

What Chesterton objects to in Hulme's philosophy is that man is not
totally dominated by fate; he has his measure of choice and free will.
While agreeing with the need for a different kind of expression he is
against infinite abstractions and the language of diagrams that Hulme
proposes. They are in an inverted way, a means of evading the
exposure of human limits by choosing an abstract mode within the
reach of man. Much later in his life, Chesterton is to review several
books by people from the group influenced by Hulme, and entitle it
'Nothing to Shout About'. [5] He will admire Pound for the use of
images more solid than abstractions, but condemn him for saying that
a 'better' world is beyond human realisation. He will admire
Wyndham Lewis for vaunting religion over materialism, and
condemn him for a spineless, non-moral approach to satire. Finally he

will ask what is the point of creating such good literature to express nothing but futility.

The surrealist movement is related to Chesterton because of a similar process of imagination rather than of conscious intellect. We have looked at Chesterton's solipsistic vision in depth; and we know from himself and others that his artistic talents while a student at Slade were often visual representations of the nightmarish tendency. Indeed several works reproduced in *The Coloured Lands*, especially the cover picture of a boy impaled on street railings, show it still in force later in his life. Jorge Luis Borges notes that:

> the powerful work of Chesterton, the prototype of physical and moral sanity, is always on the verge of becoming a nightmare. The diabolical and horrible lie await on his pages.[6]

Only in *The Man Who Was Thursday* did Chesterton have the confidence to discuss the vision, and the subtitle of that novel is 'A Nightmare'. The movement which manifests as a code of expression the fears of Chesterton is surrealism. He had a surrealist frame of mind and spent most of his life trying to control the effect of it on his imagination. C. H. Waddington points out that surrealism was a 'solipsistic vision' that attempted to make actualities a creative act of the imagination. He also quotes Madge as saying that the surrealist hallucinations and dreams were conscious. The entry on surrealism in the *Encyclopedia Britannica* also speaks of it as an intellectual and 'methodological' art form. But imagine what would happen if these hallucinations were uncontrollable, were an unavoidable part of one's approach to the world, and we come close to *Nausea* and G. K. Chesterton's mind.

It is important that surrealist art functions by analogy. It uses the juxtaposition of two unrelated objects as an active mode of communication. Waddington speaks of Jean Brun stating that the discovery of surrealism was that 'the word *comme* is a *verb* which does not signify *telque*'. The fundamental function in Chesterton's ideas on communication is this active act of analogy. It is as if he took the analogical function which was at the root of his fears and turned it inside out to prove that fear impossible. Instead of seeing interminable analogies derived from his own mind, he views the world as full of analogies derived from God's mind. One is reminded of the observation in *Robert Browning* that Browning's mysticism:

was not of that idle and wordy type which believes that a flower is symbolic of life; it was rather of that deep and eternal type which believes that life, a mere abstraction, is symbolic of a flower. (183)

Robert Browning made the man in more ways than one.

The closeness of Chesterton's views to the surrealist and later absurdist outlook is demonstrated by the interpretation imposed on *The Man Who Was Thursday* by a communist theatre group. Rather than treating the book as anti-anarchist, they staged it as an anarchist play. Similarly the very structure of Chesterton's mystical style lends itself to a style that intends to negate mysticism. While he attempted to convey the existence of a divine presence in his work by indicating something beyond his expression, the fact that 'something beyond' is only indicated leaves open the possibility of 'nothing beyond' being indicated. In the examination of nonsense it became clear that the mode could be used to indicate either some real basis or nothing. Either way, it is not an ultimately satisfying mode because it is controlled by the rules of one man. Allegory allows the unknown to participate in the mode. It is not merely a technical conceit. For a mystic this makes the mode far more meaningful, for God may enter the work. Just so, for an absurd poet the mode may be reversed in its intention by making it possible for an unknown to enter, but denying the possibility of its existence. In this way, the sense of 'nothing' is made far stronger and more terrible.

The path that Chesterton was trying to hold between these two extremes of total determinacy and total liberty was peculiar to himself and in 1908, to only a few others. It was a path difficult to follow since both the extremes and the middle way had in common a rejection of the current modes of symbolic and discursive communication in their impressionist and rationalist forms. Chesterton resolved his problem by finding in the mystic relationship with God, which also contained a social function, the concept of the mystic artist. There were others with similar approaches. We should remember Wilde's insistence on the use of the concrete form to express essence, and his belief in the importance of the mystical in revealing truth. Paul Valéry's work not only agrees with the necessary social function of the mystic, but also points to the central aspect of mystical expression as separating yet fusing thing and instinct. Later on, men such as Jacques Maritain, the Abbé Brémond and David Jones were to expand upon this idea of the mystic artist and his modes of expression. However, that Chesterton would not have been able to, or not prepared to recognise the contributions of these men, only underlines his difficulty at the time of writing *Orthodoxy*.

It is unavoidably noticeable that most of these people were Roman Catholic in practice or in tradition, and it is probable that Chesterton shares with them an element common to their Catholic faith. Whereas the secularisation of Christian imagery has often been discussed with reference to the early twentieth century, it is important to recognise the vitality of its internal structure. The sacramental structure is still used for expressing the inexpressible, the beyond man, the mystic presence, whether or not it be the Christian God. In Chesterton's eyes the specifically catholic nature of authority allows for an energy in art which is not destructive because it breaks out from within specific limits and laws, yet it is satisfying and cathartic. The paradoxical nature of Christianity, as he saw it, also makes language very important because misuse of it could destroy the tension of opposites that creates and transcends limits. Significantly Chesterton says that Catholic Christianity also makes possible the 'living' of poetry as if life itself were the highest expressive form.

ii

The ideas about mysticism and the mystic as artist are inherent in *Orthodoxy*, but the sophistication that Chesterton was later to develop is not. While he has established the new positive approach for his religion and art, he still has to work out of his system the confusions of a decade. Significant changes are still to come in both his religious conversion and his development of allegory. There are two major aspects of art in *Orthodoxy* which are emphasised and still recall the direction of the earlier thinking: the necessity for will in order to limit and control, and the need to pierce to the essence of a thing at the expense of its material covering. The points both arise from Chesterton's concluding statement on his belief that 'personal creation [will] is more conceivable than material fate'. Even though he briefly points to Nietzsche and Tolstoy as examples of too great an intellect and will, this is not stressed. It as though he were still not completely aware of the difference between personal will, and will inspired and controlled by belief in God.

However, in *George Bernard Shaw* and *William Blake*, the critical works of 1909 and 1911, he begins to concentrate heavily on the potential for will to become self-directed, not divinely directed. As he noted but did not fully examine in *Charles Dickens*, the limitations imposed by an artist may distort the essence of a thing and the communication degenerate into self-centred fantasy. Similarly his early praise for Plato as a man not dominated by the material is tempered a little in *Orthodoxy* when Plato with Emerson is used to exemplify human understanding, as against the divine understanding of the Church. In *George Bernard Shaw* a comparison with Plato is used to define Shaw as a human idealist to be commended for the fight against 'materialism', but denounced for the neglect of material form that allows the personal version of the essence. It is important to note the relationship between these two shifting aspects of Chesterton's thought because they partially explain each other. As the author becomes more aware of the dangers of self-directed will, so the external form of things becomes important because it places limits on human distortion. *Orthodoxy* introduces in a simple example the origins of Chesterton's growing respect for Aristotelian thought. He briefly mentions the necessity for the '$\mu\varepsilon\sigma o\nu$' principle. Walking the 'middle way' is impossible without recognising the limits as to how far one can move on either side. In later works he also becomes aware of Aristotle's appreciation of the material form of things as a positive limiting factor, not as the degenerate 'materialist' viewpoint that he had previously understood it to be.

The critical work *George Bernard Shaw* discusses the two points, and the background provided for them clarifies Chesterton's change towards a positive belief. The first of the three categories under which Shaw is examined is 'The Puritan'. It is here that the central criticism originates. The puritan has a direct and personal relationship with God. His expression of the divine is intellectual, based on explaining things in the light of personal understanding which is for him absolute truth. His approach to objects is to perceive this absolute divine essence in them making the appearance less important. On a political level Shaw the puritan is a republican. In a republic theoretically nothing lies between the people and the government. Democracy, on the other hand, uses the process of representative government which interposes a candidate between people and government. In his philosophy the intellectual confidence of knowing absolute truth allows Shaw to directly attack any problem. As a writer, his concern with the ideas rather than the word makes him a precise logician in style.

Ultimately Shaw's love for art is also defined by the ability of a specific mode to communicate directly with him. Chesterton suggests that Shaw's appreciation of music is twofold. Firstly there is no limiting form between himself and meaning; and secondly music seems to convey the meaning precisely, and without distortion. Music apart, Shaw's awareness of the imprecision of other modes of art allows him to separate their fictions from reality. In this he is a mystic, caring more for morality than art. In Chesterton's view he cares more for the acknowledged limitations of art that will express morality in the relationships of things, than for creating art as an object only valuable in itself. However he is a 'black and white' mystic, believing in his knowledge of absolute truth. While the critic gently reprimands Shaw saying, 'But black and white are not the only two colours in the world', he adds:

> Nevertheless, it is a good thing that the more austere method should exist separately, and that some men should be specially good at it. (158)

Shaw's specifically puritan background negates the most important value in Chesterton's central idea of Christianity: the holding of seemingly opposite forces in tension. It is where the critic examines the implications of the negation that he begins adversely to criticise his subject. The criticism is summed up in the discussion of paradox. There are two stated uses of paradox. The first indicates an apparent inconsistency, and the second a verbal contradiction. Shaw only uses the first:

> He does not allow for the deeper sort of paradox by which two opposite cords of truth become entangled in an inextricable knot. (182)

The second use, as a contradiction, demands belief; the first however, holds within it the potential for explanation on which Shaw insists. While Shaw believes in the sanctity of will to explain things, it is the sanctity of human will. Man's own divine capacity for creation and choice become in the end higher than external authority. The result is that man's theories about things become more important than the unalterable 'essence' of the things themselves. The progress of Chesterton's thought on this problem is very important. It is his first reasoned account of the difference between dogmatist and didactic. What was a confusion in *G. F. Watts* and implied in *Heretics* is here examined and clarified. Shaw's paradox is shown to be wrong because it is the dominance of a personal opinion not externally

inspired. Contradictory paradox however, in demanding belief
contains the external. It is the simultaneous existence of inspiration
and dogma. The fact that Chesterton has worked out the basis not
only for his approval but also for his disapproval is a sign of the
maturity of his criticism.

As a result of the belief in the sanctity of his own will, Shaw is
capable of creating 'his own vast and universal religion'; but only he
belongs to it. Similarly, although Shaw is a republican, he finds his
own republic the best and the contribution of other individuals is lost.
The most influential effect is found in his writing. Chesterton notes
that he is incapable of writing 'problem' plays because he always has a
need to explain. Because he has no tradition he cannot understand the
function of symbol in relation to truth. It interferes with, rather than
clarifies, meaning. Because he does not believe in representative art,
he cannot interpret the allegory of fairy-tales. Finally, because he
needs always to explain, he will tend to impose his own theories upon
things whose 'idea' or essence he cannot fully understand.

The direction of Chesterton's criticism is towards assessing the
value of Shaw as a mystic artist. The need for 'black and white'
mystics is that they completely separate the spiritual and material.
However, as previously noted there is also a responsibility to
communicate their understanding of the meaning of the separation
which transcends the division. Just as Shaw often tends to separate too
far a thing and its essence, interposing his theory of it, so his style often
does not communicate adequately. Logic is not enough. Chesterton
says that to communicate one must have a connection with people, a
tradition, a ritual. The essays of this period continually mention the
importance of a popular style, the use of chorus to humanise a story,
the genuine vitality in dialect and slang, and the role of the poet in
expressing the ideas of the populace. Shaw only succeeds as a mystic
artist when the characters of his plays are able to communicate with
the people. This happens when his personal impressions of characters
coincide with divine revelation. At these times one:

> can see shining and shaking through them at that instant the
> splendour of the God that made them and of the image of God who
> wrote their story. (216)

The critic finds that the coincidence usually occurs when Shaw is for a
moment emotional, and the iron control over his human will lapses
slightly to admit weakness. Without this necessary admission of

inadequacy mystic truth cannot be communicated, because mystic truth must indicate an absolute external authority.

Chesterton's interest in aspects of mysticism continues in the critical work *William Blake*. One of the first points that is made is that Blake is Irish. The Irish, according to the critic, are logical. The second point he makes is that Blake is a mystic, 'a man who separates heaven and earth even if he enjoys them both'. Not surprisingly the book takes the same critical direction as that on Shaw, Shaw as also being a logical Irish mystic, and it attempts to assess the value of Blake as a black and white mystic artist. However, probably because he is speaking of a man whom he could not have known in the detail he knew Shaw, Chesterton places the emphasis on mysticism, what it is and is not, rather than on the personal factors that contribute to the kind of a mystic the subject will become.

The role of the mystic is carefully defined by distinguishing mysticism from the mysterious. It is the mystic's function to clarify the riddles of the world, to find and express the meaning of the relationship between the actual and the idea:

Every stone or flower is a hieroglyphic of which we have lost the key; with every step of our lives we enter into the middle of some story which we are certain to misunderstand. The mystic is not the man who makes mysteries but the man who destroys them. The mystic is the one who offers an explanation which may be true or false, but which is always comprehensible. (132)

Arising out of the importance first of communication, and second of communication of a reality connecting the essence and matter, are certain stylistic demands. Communication in art must be effected through a clarity and definiteness of colour and shape that makes the object being drawn unmistakeably recognisable. The form of clarity is dependent on the skill of the artist and the ideas he perceives. Mystic art must be the opposite to impressionism: It puts what one knows above what one notices; and it must also oppose rationalism: What one knows is what one reasonably believes, not what one rationalises intellectually.

Blake is a mystic in the primary sense of coming out 'to teach rather than to learn'. He tried in his elaborate organisations of ideas and energies to establish a meaning for the relationships between all things. His art fits Chesterton's definition of mystical art because it concentrates on 'the firm line', and the critic suggests that what Blake

would have hated most in art would be the vagueness of impressionism. His poetry also uses a definite form that fuses the material
and the essence. Chesterton notes that when Blake uses an image like
the lamb to represent innocence he really meant that there is 'an
eternal image called the Lamb', and that 'eternal innocence is an actual
and even awful thing'. The images did not 'stand for' innocence as an
emblem would; it does not generate an experience of innocence as a
symbol would; it presents innocence through pointing by analogy to
its absolute existence. Chesterton elsewhere describes the allegorical
function as a fusion of both the emblem and the enigma; it produces 'a
moral value. It figures forth in emblem and enigma, the truth. . . .'[7]
Because it acknowledges its own limitation in analogy to the eternal,
it makes the enigma of the eternal more actual.

The importance of Blake's allegorical form is described in passage
that compares him with Beardsley. Beardsley is called a 'decadent
mystic' who produces effect by distorting either the appearance or the
idea of a thing. Chesterton calls him 'fantastic' with a negative
emphasis. On the other hand, Blake produces effect by exaggeration
of the appearance and idea which Chesterton calls true caricature. By
means of exaggeration which is his as it was Dickens's allegorical
form, Blake transcends the matter and spirit division, for he 'saw the
image of God under all garments'. His greatness lies in his ability to
make the concept of God actual, to portray the ideal as being 'as solid
as a giant'.

But Chesterton finds himself at odds with other aspects of Blake's
art. Significantly, he ascribes these aspects to Blake's insanity.
Throughout the book there are references to artistic failures due to a
forgetting of the material appearance of the object. These accumulate
to testify to a breakdown in the mystic's material and spiritual duality
and concentrate solely on the idea. The statement is made that Blake
'held that what we call the ideal is not only more beautiful but more
actual than the real'. A corollary was that the artist denied the
authority in the pure existence of nature and material things. Since the
ideal was more important than the physical, it was a short step for
Blake to insist that 'man as an image of God had a right to impose
form upon nature'. It is revealing that Blake's factual God was also a
'personal God', in the sense of Shaw's puritan God. Blake would be
just as open as Shaw to all the mistakes arising out of a belief in
absolute human understanding.

Blake's use of images in themselves does not prove his madness; it
was essential for the production of allegory. But the one thing that

testifies to his madness in the critic's eyes, is his allowing the image to conquer the identity of a thing, allowing it to take over his artistic function. Chesterton thinks that where he went wrong was 'as an intellectual and not as a poet'. He applied his own ideas to external situations without seeking their own meaning and identity; he became a 'hard theorist', bowing to the law of his own 'outlawed logic'. In doing so he ceases to be an artist; he disregards the enigma of life, and becomes 'entirely, instead of only partially, separated from the people'. The process is an explicit example of what Chesterton fears for the mystic. As he exercises too great a personal control he attempts to avoid the existence of his limitations, to become God. Stylistically, he attempts absolute communication of the idea which is impossible since man cannot create *ex nihilo*. As a result his art fails. The corollary is also true: if art fails to communicate, it indicates a spiritual lapse. The social function of the mystic therefore guarantees his sanity.

The book *William Blake* reiterates Chesterton's belief that while the denial of 'materialism' is valuable, the disregard of the material can lead to a thing being separated from its essence. The critic has also realised that the black and white mystic, who entirely separates heaven and earth, is peculiarly open to this disregard. He never allows the connection of the material and spiritual; only portraying them as existing simultaneously but not transcended. The material places necessary limits on the understanding of the essence by the mystic, and the highest spiritualism is to affirm those limits and that material. If the object is separated from its essence the idea becomes human theory forced onto identity, which is Chesterton's concept of degenerate fantasy: debased Platonism. Man places himself in the position of God and either recognises his failure and is criminal in continuing in that position, or he goes mad. The artistic question is still the original one; how far can man exercise his creativity without blaspheming and claiming to be God? But Chesterton has now gone a long way towards answering it in personal terms.

The studies of Shaw and Blake express Chesterton's respect for, yet qualification of, the powers of the black and white mystic; but also hint at another form of mysticism. He makes a statement in *George Bernard Shaw* that the English half-believe their fiction; yet the logic of the Irish makes them completely separate the two. *William Blake* contains a second statement about English mystics like Shakespeare and Keats, and Irish ones like Blake. The English mystics, who are in Chesterton's view non-Platonic writers, fuse yet simultaneously separate the material and spiritual, whereas the Irish only separate the two. It is important to realise that the author's criticism of the Irish is here criticism of the Irish puritan. In William Blake he notes that their traditions and allegories are intellectual, based on the law and the military; as such they may always lose their traditional value and be reduced to mere logic. It helps to look at the description of the Irish Catholics in *Irish Impressions* to assess the positive values that he seeks in the English mystics. The Irish Catholics, because they are subordinate to God, can write poetry. Their tradition is Catholic Christianity, a non-intellectual ritual which cannot be reduced to human logic alone. It always maintains vital traditional values and therefore cannot lose touch with the people. It is the use of Christian ritual which maintains traditional values and social communication that Chesterton sees in the English mystics, and that provides the basis for understanding his second kind of mystic.

Chesterton has progressed from saying in *Orthodoxy* that the analogy in allegory is necessary for adequate expression of external authority, to saying that ritual is necessary so that allegory is not debased into self-centred fantasy. Further, he states that the Catholic creed is the only one able to provide an authority that can transcend the analogical limitations of both allegory and ritual in sacrament. But in Chesterton's eyes Christianity goes even further: because it allows man to live poetry, the pure artist becomes the living man, the fusion of religion, morality and expression. His life is his art, it needs no material transformation. Yet, while this is possible in the life of a saint, for example, Chesterton makes clear that it is not a path for the average man. It is also on the basis of living poetry that Chesterton says that the greatest artists are unconscious of their symbols, what they take for granted is more important than what they say. Because they do not consciously control, there is no danger of distortion through the imposition of individual theories. Yet the art would be careless and potentially immoral if there were no Christian sacramental background unconsciously present. The attitude causes him to call Milton:

> an almost solitary example of a man of magnificent genius whose greatness does not depend at all upon moral earnestness, or upon anything connected with morality. His greatness is a style, and a style which seems to be unusually separate from its substance . . . In all this I am in a sense arguing against myself; for all my instincts, as I have said, are against the aesthetic theory that art so

great can be wholly irreligious.[8]

However, Chesterton realises that mystics, who have a duty to communicate, are not pure artists and neither are they great artists. They must necessarily use the analogical mode of communication. Indeed he realises that most people are neither pure nor great artists; and therefore most people have a responsibility to control consciously through an analogy which does not distort truth; most people have to exercise a critical faculty with the artistic to ensure the communication of their perception. Chesterton knows that he too is neither a pure nor a great artist. What he has is a totally unpretentious belief that he has some mystic knowledge to convey about the wonder of the world; and he has arrived, in his development of allegory to verbalise ritual, at a mode which he thinks will convey this truth without distortion.

7 Encampment: 1912—1918

The idea that the pure artist expresses his meaning through living is one that Chesterton explores at length in the novel *Manalive*. He places the pure artist in tandem with the mystic artist. The former is unconscious of verbal meaning, expressing his identity through ritual actions. The latter is conscious of a need to find a mode to express the nature of identity, and communicate his understanding of it verbally. Chesterton combines the pure artist who has no verbal obligations to society, and the mystic artist who must communicate analogically through sound, speech or matter. The two artists each extend one half of the duality of the artist found in *The Man Who Was Thursday*. The pure artist is primarily creative, while the mystic artist primarily interpretive.

The background of Chesterton's previous novels helps to explain the division between the artist and critic in *Manalive*. Early in his career we encountered the dissatisfaction with emblem which led to an inclusion of metaphor in 'The Wild Knight'. A greater control over metaphor was exercised in *The Napoleon of Notting Hill* as if the author were aware of its potential power. The awareness was reflected in the parallel social actions he explored in the novel. However, the initial drive is there. Although emblem is unsatisfactory it is used because it directly stands for an external; it indicates the artist's limitations even if it lessens his power. To prevent emblem itself from being personally distorted Chesterton attempted to use allegory in *The Ball and the Cross*. He tried to use the emblem with the enigma in the character of Michael, but failed because the allegory was not clear. *The Man Who Was Thursday* is exciting because one can sense Chesterton's recognition of the danger in playing with forms he has rejected as anarchic. The emblem of the first three chapters and the ritual of the last three encloses the danger of these anarchic forms. But it is the ritual that provides the meaning in the book and the satisfaction.

Finally it was Syme's critical side which interpreted Sunday's analogy and found meaning through the revelation at the end of the novel. The revelation also gave him an identity that justified the value of his own artistic symbols. The criticism of the intervening years until 1912 and *Manalive*, led Chesterton to see the Christian 'living' artist as the only man with pure expression. He goes on to acknowledge that the role is suited to few men, and that the primary expression will usually be through a material language such as paint, or words. What is important about *Manalive* is that it is a statement of the author's firm belief in his own need of verbal communication, and in his role of man as a literary artist and critic. It not only sets the pattern for all his later work, but also includes within it the root of his mature political, social and critical thought.

The novel is divided into two equal parts, the first beginning with a group of people in a guest-house. Their community is suddenly interrupted by the arrival of Innocent Smith, an old school friend of one of the guests. His vast energy and unorthodox celebration of life turn the routine of the house into a series of hilarious games. Having spent a day with the guests doing ridiculous things, Innocent proposes to one of the women. The proposal so annoys and worries a close friend that she sends for a psychiatric doctor to commit him. Soon after, she too is caught up in the wild spirit of the day which results in a rush of proposals, all the guests being paired off. However, the psychiatric doctor arrives with another doctor anyway. The first thing to happen is Innocent's apparently shooting at the doctor. At this point a long discussion takes place about what they should do. The two doctors claim that they have evidence which would allow them to take Smith away and put him in an insane asylum. However, Michael Moon the other most prominent character in the novel, persuades them to hold a trial at the house. The second part of the book consists of Smith's trial on four counts, defended by Michael Moon and prosecuted by one of the doctors. The trial ends with his acquittal; but the novelist, rather than conclude in such an abrupt manner, finishes weakly on a sentimental note with advice to those about to be married.

Innocent Smith and Michael Moon are the two main characters. Smith is more simple a figure because he 'is'; he always expresses a consistent identity. Moon, on the other hand, changes his position during the course of the novel. The reader is introduced to Smith by way of a telegram which he sent to his school-time friend Arthur Inglewood. The telegram reads: 'Man found alive with two legs'. The message is enigmatic, reminiscent of Sunday's messages to the policemen in *The Man Who Was Thursday*. As with those messages, this one is interpreted individually by each different character, and the interpretations indicate a lot about the character in question. The psychiatric doctor Warner, who is briefly visiting at the beginning of the book, says rationally 'Even a baby does not expect to find a man with three legs'. Significantly, when Smith appears tumbling over the garden wall he is 'a figure like a flying wheel of legs, as in the shield of the isle of Man'; the figure on the shield has three legs. From the start Warner has condemned himself by being too logical, by excluding the non-rational possibilities and trying to explain everything with his own human understanding.

Once Smith has arrived there are many details about him which we can place and interpret, but the novelist refrains from any direct explanation of the character. Innocent is incredibly active, running around the garden, climbing trees and leaping about after lost hats. His activity leaves him little time for words; his speech is broken, fragmented, only containing the words essential to suggest meaning with few articles and connectives. He also speaks in rhyme; and one should note the importance of this to Chesterton. He says elsewhere that energy is an attempt at harmony; if we were 'real enough we should all talk in rhyme'. Later in Chesterton's career the appreciation of song becomes a more sophisticated argument that rhythm is a moral description of similarity; rhyme itself is the perfect expression of dogma in that it communicates identity. When Innocent is asked who wrote his song he says 'No one will ever write it'. It is his natural expression.

On the morning after his arrival Smith begins to create practical jokes. He turns each person's hobby into an institution. In the end all the institutions collapse except that about the High Court of Beacon. This Court was the idea of Michael Moon who makes it a parody of English law; yet while Moon carelessly throws off the idea, Smith takes it seriously; and he recognises its potential as ritual, its serious meaning in practice as its pronounces justice. He argues for its traditional value which Moon degrades with a cold intellectualism. Despite the novelist's refusal to explain, we know from all the details and actions that Innocent is nameless, a ritualist, stripped of usual expression, very physical, and breaking all conventional habits and interpretations: much like Chesterton's qualifications for the pure 'living' artist. It is not surprising then that when his name is found out at the end of Part One it is 'Manalive'.

The identification of Innocent which is by Michael Moon lies at the end of a series of revelations. If one follows them they not only establish Smith's meaning but also define Moon himself. The reader is introduced to Moon as a cynical Irishman; he is a failed barrister and now a journalist. The first clue to his character comes from his interpretation of the enigmatic telegram. He does not take it literally but immediately searches for a meaning beyond the superficial nonsense. The second insight results from his impulse to understand Innocent Smith when he appears. While Warner says nothing and Inglewood feebly suggests that Smith must be his old school friend, Moon is asking him what he does for a living, and what his purpose is. Later that night Moon and Inglewood end up on the roof of the house discussing their lives and the Irishman describes his initial state of mind as impulsive but 'tame', caught by convention and habit, hugging a routine.

The day of practical jokes introduces the 'trumph of crisis' in the form of Innocent Smith. Crisis demands choice, and choice means exercise of will and discovery of identity. For Moon, the crisis is centred around the High Court of Beacon. The choice he has to make is whether he should take it seriously, as Smith does, or not. The course to this decision forms much of the first half of the novel. After Smith's proposal of marriage, Moon is asked what he thinks of him. He answers that Smith is sane while the rest of them are mad. He says, 'Madness does not come by breaking out, but by giving in; by settling down in some dirty, little self-repeating circle of ideas; by being tamed'. Civilisation's conventions are responsible for distortion of real boundaries and identities. When asked if what he has said is true, he replies, 'Not literally true of course . . . only really true. An allegory, shall we say? a social satire.' Yet the fact of Smith's sanity is true, and needed to be verbally communicated through allegory to be understood.

Moon's next perception is that Smith is practical, that his practical jokes were valuable actions that represented truth. While Moon has been working this out, Smith's presence has also affected the other characters. They have all proposed to each other, and now in celebration they dance. At first each individual moves separately in 'leaps and pulsations of objectless energy', and they dance together 'half laughing and quite ritually'. Their dance is the expression of Smith's effect on them; a simple, physical ritual of joy. It breaks up suddenly when Dr. Warner reappears to take Smith away.

During Warner's search for Smith, Moon expands humorously on what he thinks Smith is. He suggests that he is the embodiment of youthful inspiration, and that:

his innocence was too close to the unconscious of inanimate things not to melt back at a mere touch into the mild hedges and heavens. (58)

Although he is right about the unconscious innocence, the idea of Smith, he is verging on the mistake of thinking that Smith does not materially exist. When Innocent appears after shooting at Warner, Inglewood's reaction emphasises the solidity of the man in a description reminiscent of the effect of mystic art:

All these things seemed unnaturally distinct and definite. They existed, like symbols, in an ecstasy of separation. (59)

While Smith's arrest is being discussed, Moon has been thinking. He has stood by the gate to the street, and now refuses to let the two doctors and Smith pass through. As if he too experienced Inglewood's feeling of wonder at the actuality of their surroundings, he suddenly recognises the possibility of a real High Court of Beacon. He is now not just intellectually but 'morally certain there's some blunder, or some joke, or some allegory', beyond Smith's shooting at Warner. After much debate, he points out that Smith could have killed them all as they stood there talking, but he has not. The common sense behind the remark 'exploded silently underneath all their minds', and they intuitively know he is innocent. The High Court of Beacon is initiated not to pass judgement but to inquire into the meaning of the man.

Before the trial begins Moon talks to Inglewood to convince him that he understands Smith. The Irishman proceeds with an extensive description of the function of analogy in allegory and ritual. The explanation starts with hieroglyphics and likens them to riddles. They are both plain in colour and shape but the meaning eludes one. Dances are similar but even harder to understand. Moon has realised that Innocent speaks very little, 'that all he really did was actions'; and says that he is figurative. Finally he comes to the conclusion that 'Innocent Smith is not a madman — he is a ritualist. He wants to express himself, not with his tongue, but with his arms and legs . . . All other jokes have to be noisy — . . . the only silent jokes are the practical jokes. Poor Smith, properly considered, is an allegorical practical joker.' In understanding Smith, Moon has been performing the function of a critic; consciously explaining the meaning of the actions. This could not have been done if the intellectual process of understanding Smith had not been supplemented by the experience of wonder at the actuality of the world which makes sense of Smith's actions. What happens to Moon at his moment of crisis is a conversion, specifically a Christian conversion. In *Orthodoxy* the five tenets of Chesterton's belief only satisfied by Christianity, begin with the statement that the world is only explained by a miracle that reveals the wonder of the world. The others follow necessarily from this. Moon experiences this wonder and is turned from an intellectual mystic into a Christian mystic. When this happens he is able to choose, and to find identity in the act of exercising externally inspired will. The ability to perform an act of will allows him to understand the concept of ritual, because they both involve a recognition of human limitation. He can therefore understand Smith and choose to express ritual through the allegory of law infused with the concept of Christian justice: to pardon a man even if guilty.

To summarise, Innocent Smith is man alive, the unconscious artist expressing meaning in living. He is the fusion of religion, morality and expression. He brought freedom to the people of the house because of the inspiration speaking through his actions. His unconscious artistic role was to provide institutions or rituals to express meaning. Those without Christian ritual collapsed; the one with it did not. Moon at first is the puritan intellectual mystic explaining logically; but after his choice he becomes a Christian mystic admitting the non-rational and understanding religious ritual. His role is conscious; he is partly critic not pure artist, and he communicates his understanding of meaning and value through the conscious allegory of Christian justice. The relationship of Smith and Moon can be clarified with reference to an essay called 'The Thing'. While Chesterton insists elsewhere that all good ideas seek embodiment, he warns against following form out of habit's sake. He says that:

> The vitality and recurrent victory of Christendom have been due to the power of the Thing to break out from time to time from its enveloping words and symbols. Without this power all civilizations tend to perish under a load of language and ritual.[1]

Smith is the 'Thing' that breaks out, while Moon is the mystic artist who tries to communicate through inspired allegory.

Part One of *Manalive* was entitled 'The Enigmas of Innocent Smith'. Innocent's behaviour is that of an enigma, figuring forth

truth through his actions; and the chapters present the responses of all
the characters to something that they do not completely understand.
The second part of the novel is appropriately called 'The Explanations
of Innocent Smith'. In it the characters, having recognised the
existence of truth, try to assess what that truth is. The trial that takes
place is a battle between the forces of pure intellect and those of
Christian mysticism. The doctor who represents the prosecution is a
rationalist. The restriction of his logic to merely human understanding is an example of what intellectual mysticism can be debased to,
and the prosecution evidence obscures rather than illuminates
meaning. Michael Moon the defence lawyer, argues on the basis of 'a
fellow's religion'. As far as he is concerned all 'facts' may be
individually interpreted; the only absolute meaning for them must lie
in referring to an external authority. In presenting his evidence Moon
emphasises the personal perspective to introduce a partially objective
viewpoint by exposing the prejudice or personal limitation that is
there.

Each charge revolves around an aspect of the Christian mystic.
Indeed the first piece of evidence presents two points of view, that of
ritual action and of allegorical explanation. The division underlines
the point that without the actions the meaning would be valueless and
vice versa. The initial charge is that Smith shot at the Warden of
Brakespeare college; and the defence is that he did so not to kill but to
wake the Warden up to the fact that he wanted to live. Primary in the
mind of the Christian mystic is the worth of life, that makes suicide an
ultimate sin. The second charge is that he stole things from houses;
and the defence is that he only stole from himself. During the
evidence it is noted that Innocent's:

> creed of wonder was Christian by this absolute test; that he felt it
> continually slipping from himself as much as from others. (140)

He stole from himself because he needed to affirm the importance of
the things he owned.

Having proved the value of life and things, the third and fourth
charges prove the value of home and marriage. The third case
produces four letters in evidence that he abandoned his home, but
they add up to the fact that he left home in order to return. The
prosecution says that the letters are 'fairy-tales', and so they are in that
they communicate through allegory an absolute fact. The last charge,

of bigamy, is resolved by proving that Smith keeps remarrying his own wife to keep the value of their marriage alive.

Moon's conclusion is that Innocent has a 'spiritual power' to distinguish 'between custom and creed. He has broken the conventions, but he has kept the commandments.' Although he seems to have broken tradition what he has really broken is outmoded habit. Because he is Christian and can 'live' poetry, his life sustains true tradition. Moon's legal allegory in the form of a detective story, expresses the meaning of the living ritual. The allegories of evidence used within the form of the trial are means of communicating his understanding of Innocent's actions. But, although the mystic can present the logic of the actions, a final acceptance of the justice of the pardon cannot be made without belief in the Christian creed. As he has said, it is only with reference to the external authority of God that the evidence carries absolute value.

The communication on a narratorial level parallels that within the story. Chesterton as a novelist avoids the use of symbol and in separating the two parts of the book into enigma and explanation he is not only reaffirming his use of allegory but also demonstrating both Underhill's categories of the allusive and descriptive techniques of the mystic artist. The first half of the novel is a mixture of emblem and riddle. There are brief impressionistic passages to create a feeling of uncertainty, and longer descriptive sections about the actions of the characters, but they are not as dominant as the other elements. He uses emblem to establish the conventions from which the characters must be released, and the names of the characters are indicative if not totally explanatory of their personalities. The second part is a mixture of Moon's connecting descriptions and the evidence. All the allegories function on the narratorial level as well, and just as the allegories speak for Smith, so they speak for Chesterton.

If we relate the ideas of the novel to the philosophy of the novelist, most of the concepts stated in *Orthodoxy* are apparent. Most important is the idea of revelation, that Moon understands only through some miracle suddenly happening to him. Together with this is the idea of identity, that man can only know himself if provided with revelation. Moon's understanding of Innocent is coincident with new knowledge, which he then has a responsibility to communicate. The revelation takes place in the first half of *Manalive*, and the communication of understanding in the second. The division of the book reflects the mystic duality of essence or spiritual showing itself in material, and the human aspect relating to the divine. Just as the mystic must include both, yet separate them, in the complete existence of the novel Chesterton has fused the essence with the material, the enigma with the explanation, yet kept them apart. The fusion is in the creed that lies behind the philosophy, just as the belief in the creed was the only basis for Moon's justification of Innocent. What should be noted, and will be expanded on later, is that *Manalive* is fundamentally the form for all Chesterton's detective stories. The detective story becomes an allegory for him to communicate through because it so clearly contains the elements necessary for his expression of Christian ritual.

Throughout Chesterton's early work the novels have reflected the dominant concerns of the critical enquiries. Not only have they reflected but often clarified the intent by restating the critical confusions in terms of conflicting characters and styles that are partially resolved. Just so *Manalive* summarises the developments in thought that arose out of *Orthodoxy*, and clarifies the discussion of the role of the mystic artist which the critic developed in later works. At this stage in his career Chesterton had reached a peak of popularity and success. Further, he had generously defined a philosophy for himself that was satisfying and stimulating in its breadth. The result in *The Victorian Age in Literature* is probably the best example of early Chesterton as essayist, literary critic and moral commentator.

The Victorian Age in Literature is a broad application of the need for ritual expression in art, but the author also extends the need for ritual expression in art into the fields of politics and society. Chesterton begins by examining what he calls the Victorian 'compromise'. The compromise consists initially of two forces: the middle classes coming to a compromise with the existence of the aristocracy, and the aristocracy deciding to recruit new members from the middle classes. The social expression which results has three evils: puritan politics without puritan theology; constitutional patching up; and admiration for industrial wealth. In Chesterton's terms this meant limited intellectual thought, outworn conventions, and a vulgar materialism dependent on the suppression of the masses. Ultimately it resulted in 'the cheapness and narrowness of its conscious formulae; the richness and humanity of its unconscious tradition'. The statement denounced not only the Victorian style of living, but also their style of art.

The analysis of Macaulay is essentially an analysis of the Victorian compromise in action. It begins by saying that there were two Macaulays. The rational Macaulay was the result of 'dull parliamentarism' which fostered a small and narrow consciousness. Politically he believed in the concept of progress, of things getting better. The attitude reflected the Puritan ideal of absolute human perfection, and tended to disregard tradition. He also advocated complete toleration which backed up the utilitarian theory of everyone with a perfect niche for maximum happiness, which is man-imposed fate and a debasing of puritan 'predestination'. On the other hand, the romantic Macaulay had a 'festive antiquarianism', a greatness of mind that possessed a passionate love of history and tradition; and an enthusiasm for wild risks and great occurrences. In the event the small Macaulay conquered the great. He gave way to the presence of Benthamism which became the central Victorian philosophy, containing no spiritualism or mysticism. Chesterton's study of Victorian literature, which follows the analysis of Macaulay, discusses the attacks each author made on the utilitarian centre of Victorianism, and the failures that resulted, socially because they completely separated the masses from the government and artistically because they separated their matter from their style.

At heart, Chesterton presents the Victorian compromise as a perversion of puritanism. He justifies his discussion of the dominant creed in his introduction. 'Mere chronological order', he says, '. . . is almost as arbitrary as alphabetical order'. Artists must be linked to their morals and creeds because 'with other creeds they would have been, for literary purposes, other individuals'. The separation between matter and spirit, masses and government, began with the puritan creed. In Chesterton's eyes it is a personal creed where individual judgements and explanations are important because they reflect the inspiration of a personal God. Being identical with Chesterton's previous qualms about the Irish puritans, the ideas are open to potential despotism and distortion. The critic believes that whatever exists on the level of creed will manifest itself in life and art. Artistically, the purely intellectual control leads to a separation of the style from the content. It is potentially distorting; and since it does not communicate on a ritualistic basis to the masses, it creates an intellectual aristocracy. The art holds up the compromise in spite of its material attack on it. The separation between style and content indicates an intellectual aristocracy which sustains the idea of a political aristocracy that lies at the root of the compromise.

The central examination of the rise and fall of capitalism is indissolubly linked with a criticism of style. Chesterton was as convinced that puritanism was responsible for the rise of a capitalist aristocracy that was oligarchical and oppressive as he was that it produced a literature communicating only by human rationalism. The book examines the Victorian prose, poetry and novels to point out how, in each case, the separated style and matter caused their failure. Among the men of letters, Chesterton finds that their intellect inteferes too much. Dickens the journalist alone fused the two because 'he had no abstractions'. He was forced to communicate his attack on the compromise with the realities he understood, and in doing so unconsciously communicated what was wrong far more effectively. As a result his attack was the most successful.

The study of Victorian novels continues the idea of the fusion of style and matter as being necessary for success. The critic looks at Dickens and Thackeray as the two novelists of the period, but both, especially Thackeray, are condemned for pardoning too often. They do not insist on the judgement and limitation that might have broken the Victorian compromise. Among the poets Chesterton points mainly to Tennyson and Browning. Tennyson he laments as a brilliant poet who 'could not think up to the height of his own towering style'; he was a creature of the compromise and could not see beyond it. Browning is better off in that he at least had a profound philosophy that matched his grotesque and vivid style. But there is a reservation about his lack of knowledge on a broader plain, his concern for the personal, at the expense of social truth.

The later Victorians withdraw from the attack on the compromise. Shaw and Kipling side with the material neglecting the spiritual. The result is socialism in one, jingoism in the other, neither of which can succeed because they have no creed to sustain them. Finally it is Henry James who leads to what Chesterton wants to say. James has his thrill, 'not so much in symbol or mysterious emblem as in the balance of interventions and protections between mind and mind'. Communication without the limitation of form is impossible; the body must be presented along with the mind for the mind to have meaning. The statement that 'the presence of soul and substance together involves one of the two or three things which most Victorians did not understand — the think called a sacrament' sums up the criticism contained in the book. Sacrament is an admission of human limitation and an exercise of will; it also means using the tradition of the masses. The social statement of the book is that if one is closer to representing the masses, one must use a sacramental style; and if sacrament is used, there can be no compromise because it implies that forces are kept in a tension. Therefore if the writer is closer to the masses then there can be no Victorian compromise. The sacrament to effect the communication in art is the use of allegory based on catholic ritual, and in politics, democracy.

The criticism of Victorian literature is a summary of Chesterton's development. The writers fail as artists when they do not use allegory and ritual, thereby failing to fuse matter and spirit; they fail as politicians because they are not truly democratic. Because they will not admit an external authority they are humanly limited; they cannot maintain the essential balance of differing forces, and are forced into compromise. The basic reason that they do not use sacrament is that they are puritan. Chesterton notes elsewhere that the puritan principle was the 'anti-sacramental principle . . . It applies equally . . . to art, to letters'. [2] In Chesterton's view if the Victorians had been Catholic Christians, they would have accepted the existence of an external authority; the matter and the soul would have existed separately yet been fused in living. This would have made possible democracy and ritual, and destroyed the compromise. Chesterton's own changing religion parallels the political and artistic changes he would have liked to see. In his case it led him from liberalism to distributism, and from emblem and metaphor to allegorical expression of ritual. However these points have been exaggerated to examine Chesterton's ideas. The personal basis of the judgements is hardly stressed at all in *The Victorian Age in Literature*. The book remains one of Chesterton's best works, indicating a critical balance and a peculiarly perceptive insight into the central Victorian writers. The balance derives from a balance in his whole life which was soon to break; but the critical tenets established here provide a constant platform for the work of the next ten years.

The Flying Inn, written in 1914 on the eve of Chesterton's mental and physical breakdown, already indicates the instability that was to characterise much of his writing during the war. In it he makes his personal fear of creeds other than catholic the obvious basis for political and artistic degeneration. The opposing forces are Moslem against Christian, and East against West. The weak plot is based on the rising influence of a Moslem called Ammon who convinces an Englishman Lord Ivywood to take him on as an assistant. The first reform Ivywood makes is to close pubs. The two protagonists are a publican and his Irish friend Dalroy, who travel across England distributing their supply of rum. When the masses realise that the government is still distributing alcohol to the aristocracy they begin to fight back and it is just in time, for the Eastern powers have invaded England. The sub-plot concerns the aristocrat Lady Joan who, although tempted towards accepting Ivywood finally falls in love with and chooses the Irishman Dalroy.

The characters clearly represent the major issues of Chesterton's belief. They are not 'people' but emblems. Ammon stands for the creed of the Crescent that is based on 'the principle of perpetual growth towards an implied and infinite perfection.' Under this creed symbolism is not allowed. Because the possibility of perfection exists, nothing else will suffice. Since it is impossible for them to transcend human limitation, they will not submit to the humiliation of admitting it, and produce nothing which attempts representation. Ammon's expressive style is found in the speeches he makes. Their technique depends upon twisting the literal meaning or the sound of the words, denying their growth through the language. His habits and arguments are pointed in the direction of practicality and utilitarianism, never ritual communication and spiritual needs.

Lord Ivywood is a puritan Englishman who comes under the influence of Ammon and both the puritan and Islamic background lead him to believe in the concept of destiny. As he grows more powerful, he develops a love of fate, a belief that he was destined to be great. This becomes a belief that he can be a Nietzschean Superman. The final page of the book presents Ivywood as totally insane because he believes he is God.

As an artist Ivywood has the facility to speak exquisitely. The point is made that although he could make ideas 'blossom into verbal beauty: yet his face remained dead while his lips were alive'. There is no connection between the physical man and the words he uses. Later on he is referred to as a poet who created 'a poetry that never touched earth; the poetry of Shelley rather than Shakespeare'. It is an important detail that links him with the Platonists rather than the Aristotelians in Chesterton's mind and therefore with the potentially self-centred fantasists, not with the material mystics. Ultimately he becomes the patron of 'Post-Futurist' art in which there are no definite shapes because there can be no idols, and no sacramental allegories that admit limitation. But this art manages to avoid choice, to evade acts of will, to deny identity. Because Ivywood denies limitation he fulfils Chesterton's definition of the madman and becomes insane.

The two protagonists are far less well-developed as characters, partially because they do not verbalise much, but also because Chesterton seems to be more concerned with the dangers of what Ivywood represents, than the strength of catholic belief. Dalroy is our Catholic Irishman. He is described briefly as a 'mixture of cynicism and quixotry'. He acts rather than speaks, and communicates mainly through song. He has a combination of the characteristics of both Innocent and Moon. His friend Humphrey Pump is the 'kind' Englishman who communicates through gossip 'so allusive as to almost amount to reticence'. The insistence on their non-verbal basis contrasts strongly with continual use of words by Ammon and Ivywood. The protagonists live ritual and communicate through actions, and finally oppose active war to Ivywood's written law.

One of the more important characters is Joan. She is the only person in whom temptation to Eastern mysticism is a conscious issue. At first she is tempted by the pure beauty of Ivywood's world of art, but then realises that it has no humour. Her sense of humour is a significant characteristic because Chesterton allies it with man's humility because it can 'dethrone him from his official dignity'. Joan is also tempted by the respect she gives Ivywood for his manifestation of will; but she comes to realise that it is human will and that it is operating on her, and no human being has the right to operate his personal will on another. Finally she is tempted by the courage of the hero until she recognises that while heroism is good, hero-worship is not. Her growing knowledge of the immoral aspects of Ivywood's creed is an object-lesson in how we too should recognise the dangers; but the novelist leaves ambiguous whether she chooses Dalroy of her own accord, because the events of the book sweep her away with them.

The novel portrays the results of the creed of perfection and destiny. It leads to oligarchy, despotism, loss of tradition; to pictures with no shapes, no limits; and ultimately to madness. Against this is catholic Christianity, with its admission of limits, its humility, its mass power and tradition. The book is unsatisfying except as a crossword that fulfils Chesterton's ideas as we work out the puzzle. Stylistically it is very uneven, like a collection of individual short stories strung together by a weak plot. Ideologically the novel is also unbalanced. Although Chesterton gives dignity to the Pasha and Eastern culture, this extreme personal hatred of compromise makes the character of Ammon vile to the extent that one feels that the author's judgement has lapsed. Also the offhand fusion of Moslem and Jew is totally dishonest. Chesterton knew that the Moslem tenet of perfection was an anathema to Judaism; yet he combines the two together as if they were one. The effect of this interference of personal feeling is to reduce the validity of his fear concerning potential political and artistic degeneration. He comes very close to doing what he is continually warning against, which is the imposition of his own view on a situation without searching for its true identity.

8 New Explorations: 1918–1925

The years 1913 to 1923 yielded many books about historical, political and social criticism. These are similar to *The Flying Inn* in that they concentrate on demonstrations of the application of sacrament in all subjects. They also tend to be too stridently personal, especially in their condemnation of Germany during the Great War. The loss in critical objectivity and calibre is partly due to the stresses that led to the author's breakdown of 1914–15 when he lay in a semi-conscious state for three months. Much of the tension was created by the libel action against his brother Cecil that followed from his ill-considered exploitation of the Marconi case in his newspaper 'New Witness'. After Chesterton's recovery in 1915, he continued to dissipate his energies at 'New Witness' probably because he felt a necessity to take over the political and social criticism of his brother while he was away fighting, even though Chesterton's own abilities lay in rather different directions. However, the books of this period do bear out the solidity of his belief; and are interesting in picturing the total interdependence of all aspects of his life.

The extent of the interrelationship of religion, morality and expression is profound. Rather than meticulous argument, it is the consistency of detail throughout a vast expanse of writing that is incredible and convincing. The Catholic faith is shown to be at the root of the democratic and familial morality that stabilises society. It is also shown to inspire the ritual and allegorical aspects of his expressive mode. As his personal philosophy deepened, the intimately related use of allegory became more defined in his artistic works. Yet his critical writing also contributes theory and example to the mode. Early in this central period of his life Chesterton had outlined the mystic quest of the critic: to find 'the subconscious part of the author's mind', and to express intelligent responses to it in words.[1] He goes on to say that while the great artist may not consciously use a 'philosophical symbol', all critics as mystic artists, have to recognise them:

There can be no doubt among sane men that the critic should be allegorical. Spenser may have lost by being less realistic than Fielding. But any good criticism of *Tom Jones* must be as mystical as the *Fairie Queene*.[2]

The ways in which Chesterton constructs this allegorical expression in his criticism are best illustrated with direct textual examples.

An early image can be found in the first chapter of *Alarms and Discursions*. The author compares his 'fragments of fleeting journalism' to the 'gargoyles of a definite cathedral'. Even though he cannot connect the chaotic fragments, he places his trust in the unifying effect of the cathedral that contains them.[3] The analogy clearly points to the necessary power of God to make sense of his life; and functions expressively as the introduction to a collection of essays which also need overall guidance. The technique is found again and again in the books of the period. *Irish Impressions* is particularly full of analogy. It is always used when the author wishes to impose a feeling on his reader without which the factual background is meaningless. One clear example occurs when he wants to communicate his vehement dislike for the British Empire's swallowing smaller states like Ireland and destroying her peasantry. He begins by saying that the Empire may disintegrate because it is only a combination; the peasantry will not because it is a community. The reader is then led explicitly to compare the attack on Ireland to 'an attempt to abolish grass'. Grass is imagistically related to the peasantry in straightforward terms of their equality, multiplicity, ubiquity and 'power to return'. But then the author leaves the peasantry behind and speaks only of the grass. He says that to fight grass is to fight God and that man can only:

> so mismanage our own city and our own citizenship that the grass grows in our own streets. And even then it is our streets that will be dead; and the grass will still be alive. (44)

The image has been separated from the initial analogy, and in doing so has become enigmatic, more indicative of the spiritual consequences of the imperial attack. Analogies indicate the relationship between the spiritual and the material aspects of the discourse. Significantly they are rarely directly connected with the text; the reader must search for any connections himself, although the initial guidance comes from the author. The images are never intrinsically made one with the meaning, but placed by its side as if to suggest its identity not only by its similarity but also by its dissimilarity. Analogy functions by indicating, not representing, identity, yet because of this is paradoxically closer to identity.

In the newspaper articles this style may sometimes mislead. The power of the initial analogy, which one usually accepts, carries the acceptance over onto the content of the article which may be completely unrelated. This shows a potential for a dangerous imposition of personal will through technique, which Chesterton occasionally abuses. But the very separateness of the analogy from the content often prevents the danger from occurring. A more conscious use of analogy is found in *The New Jerusalem* of 1920. The book is filled with images such as the people's clothes, or the scenery which are given extensive and sometimes laboured analogical development to indicate the conflicting religions of the town. Happily the later works come to use analogy more judiciously and more powerfully. Just as the allegorical expression of this period of Chesterton's life is found in the analogical function of the detective story, so analogical image, anecdote and parable are the necessary and effective techniques for the allegorical expression of the writer's criticism.

The pervasiveness and consistency of Chesterton's allegorical expression indicate the stability of his philosophy. To understand either in a man so little given to general statements about himself, it is helpful to look at other theories of allegory and the basis behind them before going on to examine the more sophisticated theory which Chesterton later develops. The subject of allegory is surrounded by a mass of confusions. Only in recent years has it received the serious treatment it deserves, which is probably indicative of a growing return to its use. It is becoming obvious that allegory is an extremely complex subject. To deal with all its manifestations is virtually impossible without doing serious injustice to many of its aspects. However, there are areas of consistency, one being the thirteenth to fifteenth century Christian allegory, which in its later years gets involved in the advances of Renaissance humanism. As it does, it changes the nature not only of its technique but also of its interpretation.

Etienne Gilson has said of Chesterton that he was a Thomist by natural feeling not learning; and indeed one might say that he was a late medieval allegorist by nature not learning. Isabel McCaffrey suggests that one of the main functions of medieval Christian allegory, 'making sense' of an object, is only possible if 'an intelligible "outer" world and a sense-making "inner" world are aspects of a single divinely-designed universe'. As we have seen, Chesterton has placed himself in such a world. The analogical processes that become possible are second nature to his perception. Added to this is the position in which Chesterton finds himself, of being a Catholic in what he saw as a primarily humanist environment. Indeed he is far more conscious than were the late medieval writers of using allegory as a severely restricting counter to artistic blasphemy. They had an idea of the lengths to which humanist art could go as Sidney's 'Apologie for Poetry' points out when arguing that the poet may create *ex nihilo*. However, as McCaffrey adds, Sidney does not press this point and balances it by mentioning the fall of man. By contrast, Chesterton felt that he was constantly surrounded on all sides by the potential insanity of humanist modes.

Chesterton's exploration of the modes of nonsense, fancy, emblem and symbol, and his reasons for rejecting them, portray a man intuitively picking his way through a forest underlaid with traps; yet he does finally reach an open landscape beyond. The open vision may not be as artistically and humanly interesting as that of someone caught, say, in the noose of fantasy. But Chesterton is personally concerned with expressing the divine connection to the world, not with the world as an end in itself. His comments on other modes and final discarding of them are personal assessments he makes based on his own reactions. Yet he also acknowledges that if he were stronger of will, if he were more able to realise the divine part of his humanity, if he were less weak, these modes would be perfectly acceptable. His development of allegory produces a mode which prevents him from making the potential mistakes that he recognises in these other stylistic approaches.

Many of the fundamental confusions in critical approaches to allegory seem to rest upon the interpretation of the word 'metaphor', especially since C. S. Lewis's *Allegory of Love*. The traditional use of metaphor is the construction of an image so that it conveys part of the experience of reality by being 'like' it. Lewis himself seems to have meant 'stands for', in other words, an emblem. If we begin with the statement that 'every metaphor is an allegory in little' and go on to his definition of allegory as starting 'with an immaterial fact . . . and . . . invent[ing] *visibilia* to express them', metaphor seems to have a definitely emblematic function. This attitude is, as Lewis points out, based on a Platonic view of the world which says:

If our passions, being immaterial, can be copied by material
inventions, then it is possible that our material world in its turn is a
copy of an invisible world.[4]

The process is based on imitation and similitude, not on analogy.
Chesterton saw emblem as potentially distortable because one can
personally impose a 'visibilia' on an 'immaterial fact' and pervert its
true meaning. He too links the process with Platonism, which as we
have seen, he comes to distrust because it may present the actual as
valuable for its imitation of the invisible, rather than for its own
reality.

Not many critics of allegory follow Lewis's use of 'metaphor' to a
logical end, although some appear to be aware of a potential problem.
McCaffrey uses Lewis's vocabulary, but defines metaphor as analogy.
Allegory: The Theory of a Symbolic Mode by Angus Fletcher, recognises the danger, and throws out the word 'metaphor' completely,
straightforwardly substituting emblem for it. The one thing that all
these critics, including Chesterton, have in common, is a discarding of
the use of 'metaphor' as a word which, being 'like' reality, can carry the
potential of real experience. As such, it may be the basic internal
function of symbol, and symbol is a primarily individual and relative
experience in which the writer relinquishes some control of the word
to the reader. The critics agree that symbol is not controlled enough,
not clear enough in meaning to have anything to do with allegory
which is supposed to portray absolute truth. Similarly, this is the reason
that Chesterton rejects symbol and turns to allegory.

However, if metaphor means 'stands for' it can always carry the
potential for unreal experience, for fantasy. Lewis does not specifically point this out, be he implies it in his critical work and carries it
out in his fiction. He thinks that as opposed to symbol, which may
generate many different responses, allegory is valuable because it only
generates one. If a symbol creates only one response, it is allegory.
Lewis equates allegory and fantasy and says that they instigate a
controlled unity of approach; but he does not seem to differentiate
between work that portrays a very personal attitude to truth and
work which bases itself, as his does, on an external standard of truth.
Gunnar Urang, in an extensive survey of the fantasy of Lewis and his
contemporaries, reiterates the Platonic basis of fantasy and equates it
with allegory. The implication is that to be valuable, allegory must
be experienced, and it can only be experienced if it is fused with
fantasy.

As a result allegory need not, indeed should not, be tied to an absolute standard. This is what happens to Lewis's theory because it is not defined enough. Urang even goes so far, and it is quite allright for a Platonist to do so, as to say that allegorical experience may negate objective experience of the world. One may justifiably impose one's own idea on the world.

The problem in equating fantasy with allegory as far as Chesterton is concerned, is that fantasy is a supremely human genre. He sees it as a matter of invention, of literary technology. As such it persuades people into a specific pattern of thought and response to experience. The reader only has what is given, and what is given is limited to the man who invents. Unless the man inventing has absolute responsibility to others there will always be areas of distortion and perversion, even if he is unconscious of them. McCaffrey briefly touches on this aspect by saying that 'phantasia' is based on the material body of man. It is irrevocably shackled to objects of sense 'from which its second class images are derived'. Fantasy implies an absolute poetic creativity. Angus Fletcher's fascinating analysis of allegory, also Platonist, gives allegory this absolute fantastic power. The essential step in his allegory is turning the sign or artistic image of someone *into* that person, and conversely being able to reduce that person to an image or sign. The possibility of this occurring depends on man's ability to act as God, to create *ex nihilo*. Significantly he also notes that the process is demonic and magical. For this very potential Chesterton rejects fantasy. He doubted that any man could create responsibly without belief in the standard of an external authority. And he doubted further, that responsibility could be attained unless this external were included in the invention.

Another strand running through the criticism is the conceptual aspect of allegory. Quite often the idea of allegory is based on the belief that emblem cannot be distorted, and a definite code relating concepts to words is therefore possible. Lewis differentiates between a symbolic image which is 'real' and an allegorical image which is acknowledgedly 'fictional' and fixed by the writer. Because of this fixed quality allegory can be used to express conceptual details of absolute morality. Rosamund Tuve although acknowledging that 'bad' allegory is only emblematic, does say that language is fundamentally conceptual. Therefore allegory can be used to express subtleties of concepts. Again, Urang distinguishes allegorical images which are rigid, abstract and not ambivalent, from the more fluid images of myth. Fletcher's use of emblem as the basis for allegory leads him to see the mode as an 'encoding', a diagrammatic expression.

The conceptual strand in allegorical theory is obviously the 'support' for the idea of the validity of a fixed interpretation. However, if the emblem is not fixed, neither is the interpretation. Chesterton's initial experiments with nonsense logic showed him that emblems, conceptual figures, were not fixed in themselves; they needed something more to anchor them. In every critic above, the 'something more' is understood, if not pointed out. In some cases it is the presence of God, in others man alone. Yet except in the case of Tuve and McCaffrey, the neglect of the implications of this 'something more' closes the door on certain ideas about allegory that Chesterton opens.

We have seen how opposed Chesterton is to both the purely experiential and the purely conceptual. His view of allegory is peculiarly neither since it is based on the revelation of the divine. It is important to note how fundamentally different this is from current theories of language. Elizabeth Sewell, who has herself written much concerning the technique of nonsense, opens *The Orphic Voice* with a representative survey of a modern language dilemma which reflects a belief in a post-seventeenth century division between art and science. She points out that science is suffering from a language of logic that will not fulfil its needs. She also says that it finds poetic language inadequate. The basic thesis presented is˙that scientists do not understand the proper function of poetic language. In her eyes the choice is not between logic and mythology but 'between an exclusive mythology which chooses to overlook the body's participation and an inclusive mythology which is prepared . . . to admit the body, the notion of the organism as a whole . . .' But she leaves one with only two alternatives: prose, as an expression of experience disregarding the self, or poetry, as an expression of experience including the self. The duality she presents is one common to language philosophers of the early twentieth century. Wittgenstein's early insistence on discursive 'purity' and the distortion by the personal, is an example. One finds Suzanne Langer specifically building her theory around the poles of discursive and symbolic language, and when she finally proposes a middle ground of non-discursive symbols, they provide an analogue to rational logic and are conceptual.

In most cases, while the theories work well within their definitions, which is where they are supposed to work, they do not touch on the primary consideration of Chesterton who is searching for a form neither discursive nor symbolic because he wants to express the divine. Sewell rightly interprets Vico's insistence on myth as the ultimate human activity. Similarly Wittgenstein, at the end of his early *Tractatus*, says that discursive purity is only possible when discussing human knowledge of the world, not what is external to it such as ethics. Langer is also examining human communication when she speaks of discourse communicating the actual perception of the individual, and symbol communicating virtual experience. Yet even her discussion of ritual as the language of religion holds little in it similar to Chesterton's problem. She agrees with him that ritual is compulsive not propitiatory. She notes that ritual, like primitive expression, does not separate symbol from meaning; and that sacrament is the essential part of ritual because of this. But she attributes this to 'naive thinking', to 'externalized' fantasy, and to the dominance of the 'idea' or concept in our lives. It is important to note that fantasy, although with a different authority from allegory, also lies between the discursive and symbolic. While Chesterton, along with Lewis, Williams and others, agree that sacrament is the only means of expressing the divine, they differ from Langer in accepting as a fundamental truth that sacramental transubstantiation is actual, not virtual. God is not a concept for them. As a result the verbalising of sacrament becomes a far greater problem.

It is Chesterton's idea of the mystic artist and his wish to relate the divine to the world, that places him outside current theories of expression. Yet this is why, for our purposes, Tuve and especially McCaffrey are far more illuminating concerning allegory than the others. They speak about a society which takes for granted Chesterton's aim of expressing divinity, but which also accepts the restrictions on artistic form implied by the existence of that divinity. In an exploration into the supposed four levels of medieval Christian allegory, Tuve says that strict allegory 'brings us to the view of what we ought to believe'. Similarly McCaffrey states that allegory is based on a divinely ordered world. Belief in a divinely ordered world is at the root of Chesterton's Christian mysticism and his development of allegory. Chesterton's rejection of symbol, nonsense, emblem and fantasy is connected to their potential for man to act as god, to believe that he creates the world, to become insane. He is not saying that the modes are immoral in themselves but that they contain the potential for immorality. The function of images as 'like' or 'being' is dangerously close to absolute creation. This is why analogy which is 'parallel to' an object is so important, for parallels never meet. Tuve agrees that 'good' Christian allegory provides keys and indications. It is the suggestive and allusive, imperfect nature of allegory that is essential.

The mystic artist recognises the impossibility of perfectly recreating his experience, yet he has a social responsibility to communicate. The analogical function of allegory is precisely suited to his needs. It is based on the need to express verbally, yet the knowledge that it is impossible to express exactly what one means. McCaffrey's study of allegory in relation to Spenser discusses the problem not only with clarity, but also with an uncanny similarity to Chesterton. She says that her definition of metaphor as analogy:

> is helpful because it includes both the idea of separateness between word and referent *and* the notion of the referent's inaccessibility without the word.[5]

In Spenser's work, the narrator provides an initial guide to the interpretation through the style he uses. Yet the inevitable inadequacy means that the reader cannot know exactly what is meant and must participate in his own interpretation of the words. To communicate 'imageless though not inapprehensible' truth, the narrator must be consciously fictive. The style must therefore be obviously ambiguous, enigmatic and paradoxical. Plotlessness should be created by use of parataxis. Not surprisingly, these methods are virtually identical to those of Chesterton's mystic communication. McCaffrey also notes that the allegorist 'by providing clues to unlock the allegory's secret truth . . . confesses his awareness of the fiction's lying fictiveness'. Chesterton too is concerned with the consciously fictive nature of allegory. It allows the mystic artist not only to create situations, but also to provide their explanations within them.

Another aspect of the Christian mystic artist was his separation of the material and the spiritual. Chesterton has noted that without the inclusion of human limits the separation led to the imposition of personal theory on objects. His anxiety about the potential idolatry of the imagination is taken up by McCaffrey. She points out that once a writer attempts to create static, fixed images, he is abusing his creative process: 'imagination cannot be divorced from mutability without turning into its demonaic form, idolatry'. The allegorist deals with both the actual and visionary world, and needs limits and boundaries to avoid the idolatry arising from too definite a human expression of the spiritual in material terms. Again in words reminiscent of Chesterton, she says:

The allegorist incorporates within his fiction the two limits of art: the upward limit where fiction merges with transendent reality in vision; and a downward or inward limit where fiction touches clumsy life at her stupid work . . . In allegory, the 'philosophical' poet contrives to remind us continually of the boundaries, and therefore of the sources, of his poem. [6]

This dual role of allegory makes it a most appropriate mode for the mystic to use.

Ultimately the Christian mystic and the Christian allegorist must communicate the presence of God in order to transcend the divisions between creation and interpretation, spirit and matter. The functions of creation and interpretation are at the root of Chesterton's ideas on the use of allegory by the mystic artist. *Manalive*, which presents them in terms of enigma and explanation, can be seen as a paradigm for the allegorical imagination as he sees it working. In the novel the division is transcended by the acceptance of the Christian creed which underlies the actions of Innocent and Moon. It is interesting that McCaffrey's examination of Spenser's imaginative process is an exact duplicate of Chesterton's. Allegory is described as the unpacking of a fallen state, which unpacking contains both enigma and explanation, both the creative and interpretative processes. McCaffrey speaks of the creative function as synthetic, concentrating on the relation between fiction and the transcendent reality and dependent on human imagination and intellect. The interpretative function is analytic, dealing with the fiction and interior reality of fallen man. Just as Chesterton emphasises the importance of the interpretative process, so McCaffrey connects Spenser with the analytic function. The analytic is based on man's inability to express and depends on the transcending 'unanalyzed transparency' resulting from the indication of God.

Chesterton would fully agree with the statement that Spenser finally 'confesses; he prays; he reads the book he has not written'. The concept of confession and prayer as the ultimate aim of literature becomes increasingly important in his own work. Further, the idea that Spenser lets God write the book for him by constantly acknowledging him was Chesterton's main belief about the responsible artist. The presence of God in the 'unanalyzed transparency' of meaning is closely connected with a pervading image of Chesterton's later work: the stained glass window. Significantly, the image is an explanation for the use of analogy. Because analogy does not try to be or to be like the object, it may exist as a window through which to see the world. As such it is always limited. However, the limitation is transcended if light comes from without, through the window into the room. When God is indicated this happens, for his presence shines in through the work illuminating it with identity, showing that its limitations do not matter for an absolute exists beyond them. In *The New Jerusalem* Chesterton explains that the importance of Gothic windows is that they give shape, and 'even light itself is most divine within limits'. As a result the limiting form of analogy comes paradoxically closer to the identity of an absolute than any other mode. Eugene Vinaver comments that both Thomas Aquinas and Augustine note the same identifying power of analogy. Vinaver himself goes on to explain the process by saying:

> Just as in the light of day that filters through the rose window of a cathedral and illumines the sanctuary, mystical reality becomes palpable to the senses . . .[7]

Similarly C. S. Lewis observes that the glory of medieval art is 'that we see through it; it is a pure transparency'. The window, and specifically the stained glass window, becomes an analogy for the transcending process of analogy. It expresses precisely the effect Chesterton intended to be produced when he employed the allegorical mode.

ii

Chesterton's theory of allegory as found in both his artistic and critical works, is a development he makes to fulfil his aim of expressing his personal beliefs; and his approach to allegory was virtually simultaneous with his approach to the Anglo–Catholic church. For some time after formulating his idea of the mystic artist he applied the criteria to other writers, such as Shaw, with assiduity especially when he thought that they failed in using their own style and therefore needed guidelines such as those he had developed for himself. However, just as he avoids strict statements about literary theory, his concept of allegory is not a polemic on style. As he grows older his extraordinary humility becomes more apparent, and he restricts the application of his ideas only to those in whom he recognises weaknesses like his own. But it is not until 1922 and his conversion to Roman Catholicism that Chesterton seemed to have gained the confidence to treat many writers on their own terms. He

becomes increasingly willing to recognise the existence of the pure
artist and the great artist as men with different aims and achievements
than his. Much of his critical work in the last decade and a half of his
life is concerned with the relationship of man with religion and
humanity, and with the expression of the mystic artist in comparison
with that of the saint and the great poets.

In the biography of St Francis, written in 1923, we find a
refinement of ideas an expression. The book examines the life of a
pure artist, a man 'whose whole life was a poem'. Yet St Francis also
acknowledges the mystic responsibility to communicate his divine
experience. In the Saint Chesterton examines the existence of the pure
and the mystic artist in one man. The result is a far more elusive work
than *Manalive* which separated the two aspects, yet it is also more
straightforward and simple. The author connects the role of this
combination to that of the great poet, comparing their modes of
expression; and finally to himself as a mystic artist using allegory.

The biography begins by claiming that one must understand
St Francis both in body and soul. Other biographers have failed by
emphasising one part at the expense of the other. For Chesterton the
two aspects are essential to a life of St Francis because the Saint saw
religion as a kind of love affair, both spiritual and material. Without
understanding this, one misses the whole meaning of his life. The
spiritual and material duality is the basis for St Francis's mysticism. He
cannot be a materialist since he has to account on the one hand for
God, and on the other he is not entirely spiritual; and here Chesterton
distinguishes him from the 'bad' mystics who forget the actuality of
things. In contrast to his later followers the Fraticellis whom
Chesterton describes as 'mystics and not men . . . they would not
listen to reason', St Francis is supremely sane; and is so because he
recognises the external material world.

It is due to the physical aspect of the mysticism that the Saint felt a
responsibility to communicate. If something is purely spiritual, it is
easier to dismiss the possibility of verbalising it. But St Francis realized
that things:

> become more extraordinary by being explained . . . The mystic
> will have nothing to do with mere mystery; mere mystery is
> generally a mystery of inquity. (85—6)

Yet Chesterton stresses the immediate quality of the pure expression.
The Saint's art form is life; his expressions 'were always acts and not

explanations; and they always meant what he meant them to mean'. It is this different mode that separates him from the poet. Both saint and poet have a different approach to the divine. As a result they tell different truths. The poet will experience a brief mystical vision a 'brilliant levin-blaze', that emphasises the wonder of things by its contrast with them, while the saint walks always in divine light 'with an old familiarity'.

It is important to note here that Chesterton is making almost the same distinction between the mystic and poet and using almost identical vocabulary to that of Abbé Brémond in his famous lecture on pure poetry published in 1925. While Brémond acknowledges the similarity between mystic and poetic experience, he says that the object of poetry is 'the real and not the true', the poet is united with things not God. Further, he denies the social function of the mystic, saying that mystics cannot communicate. Chesterton, however, finds a connection between their experiences even if the emphases of their work are different. He notes that there is a kind of poet who praises:

> the act of creation. He praises the passage of transition from nonentity to entity; there falls there also the shadow of the archetypal image of the bridge, which has given to the priest his archaic and mysterious name. (87)

Both mystic and poet must bridge the gap between God and the material world, even if the former does so to indicate God and the latter to indicate the divinity of things.

The difference in emphasis between poet and saint leads to a difference in expression. St Francis's art does not exist to embody his spirit because his body is spirit embodied. As a result, 'All his action had something of the character of an allegory'. The inadequacy of verbal communication led him naturally to suggestion through gesture and pantomine, a 'sort of divine dumb alphabet'. But when he did use language the effect 'passed beyond words . . . to be completed by some ritual movement like a blessing or a bow'. Chesterton as a mystic artist himself has the same overwhelming sense of inadequacy in writing about the Saint. He speaks of the need for many signs and symbols to even hint at real meaning, the need to penetrate past the image to the idea. He apologises for the use of a grotesque image, saying that no other would make 'the fact clear', but adds 'of the intrinsic internal essence of the experience I make no pretence to write at all'. He is reduced to using 'short imperfect phrases', and speaks best in 'certain silent attitudes and actions'. However all this is better than the 'madness of mythological explanation' that poets abuse and which dissolves history. Chesterton freely admits that the expression is inadequate, that the mode is suggestive and allusive, rather than direct. However, in using it he has avoided falling into the potential mistakes of the poet, and avoided distortion of the truth by indicating rather than stating it.

During the years 1920– 36 Chesterton was still writing a phenomenal number of books, articles and essays; in the late twenties he even branched out into the medium of radio. Whereas his earlier groups of essays were explorations mapping out what was to him virgin territory, these focus more on the details of geography. In contrast to the pre-War journalism which was consolidating a belief, he now had the opportunity to examine more closely the often vague and intuitive feelings towards the effects of that belief in social, political and aesthetic terms.

The essays of this later period of his life show a preponderance of interest in art and modes of expression, often indicating a new willingness to face issues by which he had felt threatened previously. Particularly interesting is Chesterton's assessment of the different trends in contemporary art, which he forms out of his basic belief that while the great artist and the mystic artist communicate different things in different ways, there is a fundamental connection in their recognition of God. Taken as a whole, the essays provide a remarkably stable picture of his ideas with only one or two vocabulary changes.

Chesterton discusses with reference to the limits of human creativity the forms which expression should take for the mystic and the great artist if it is to become public. *The New Jerusalem* points out again the division between the 'divine purpose of a mystery' and the 'human of a myth'. He notes elsewhere that while true human creation is mythology, the mystic must deal in truth which is 'not only stronger than fiction, but often saintlier than fiction. For truth is real, while fiction is bound to be realistic.' The great artist is different from the mystic artist because the aims of art are different from those of religion. Art can only give 'permanent expression to a passing mood' which it cannot be certain is an eternal truth. The only stable expression is created by religion, when 'the truths are crystallized into a creed'. [8] The mistakes in art are made when it assumes that it alone has the 'supreme spiritual authority': that artists have the right to become divine arbiters. However, art is valuable if it recognises

human aims and limits. Chesterton states that 'in ultimate philosophy, as in ultimate theology, men are not capable of creation but
only of combination'.[9] He goes on to add that:

> whatever be the nature of creation, it is certainly of the nature of
> translation; it is translating something from the dumb alphabet and
> infantile secret language in our souls into the totally different
> public language that we talk with our tongues.[10]

The process of art as used by the mystic artist and the great artist,
involves different modes of translation but one single public and
social purpose.

The contrast between the ritualist and the fantasist as the extremes of
expression of divine and human authority is strongly present at this
time. The by now familiar properties of ritual are re-emphasised.
There is no need to explain ritual because it explains itself, and that far
better than 'definitions or abstractions'. It allows people to 'express in
gesture things that only a very great poet could express in words'.
Ritual is essential for expressing some things, for it is the only way in
which intense realities, such as marriage, can be communicated. The
mystery of ritual is best created through masquerade and mummery,
but the most powerful mode is silence, which acknowledges its
powerlessness. Opposed to this is fantasy and utopian literature. In a
comment on Barrie's 'Peter Pan' he notes how easily fantasy breeds
anarchy. This kind of utopian literature he sees as repressive because
its world is 'ruled by one man: the author of the book'. No matter
how perfect he tries to make it, his world will be 'despotic because it is
a dream; and a man is always alone in a dream.'[11] The essential base
for fantasy is sentiment; and sentiment contains the potential error of
the mode. Sentiment allows itself to be affected by the associations of
words rather than 'the intrinsic idea in things'. What this leads to are
self-indulgent feelings that neglect 'something equally real'; in other
words the feelings are not bad in themselves but in their exclusion of
and imposition on other equally valid ideas.

A fascinating article called 'Magic and Fantasy in Fiction' judges
the principles of fantastic fiction by distinguishing between miracle
and enchantment. Fantasy need not be immoral or 'demonic', but to
avoid it entails a recognition of God. Unfortunately it is all too easy
for fantasy to become diabolist, for the author to be a magician who is:

> the Man when he seeks to become a God, and, being a usurper, can

hardly fail to be a tyrant. Not being the maker, but only the distorter, he twists all things out of their intended shape and imprisons natural things in unnatural forms.[12]

By contrast, the man who fully includes God, effaces himself, and creates a miracle. Chesterton cites as an example of this the ritual of the mass, which is 'God seeking to be a Man'; and in which man himself is powerless.

However, the mystic artist is a truer comparison to the fantasist, for he too has to deal with words. Chesterton initially sets up a contrast between the two by linking fantasy with philosophy and dehumanised history which sets the 'mystic materialism of the sacramentalist' against the 'disembodied idealism of the pessimist'. The mystic, because he deals with matter and spirit, also deals with substance and symbol; each is essential to meaning. A few years later the critic comments on the sculpture of a war memorial, echoing his earlier distinction between the fantasist Beardsley and the mystic Blake. He says that the artist had sculpted a Unicorn by forcing its absolute substance into her own design. But while she had 'made something new out of the old Unicorn, . . . she had not made anything else except a Unicorn'.[13] This traditional mode makes new but does not distort. On the other hand, the same essay notes that negative abstractions are far more misleading than such 'caricatures', for they 'tend, of their nature, not merely to anarchy, but nothingness'. The fantasist tends to use diagrams and abstractions. He, like the dehumanised historian and philosopher, recreates his own truths or what he 'believed to be the truth'. Far more trustworthy than plans and diagrams that try to be accurate are pictures which 'professed to be picturesque'. The acknowledgement of artistic limitation is far more effective than the total human authority of the fantasist.

The sacramental mode of the mystic artist means that the very structures of his work are analogous to truth. Chesterton portrays this at work in Godfrey's building of Jerusalem which he compares to an allegory. He notes that the timber involved 'many of those mathematical that are analogous to moral truths, and almost every structural shape has the shadow of the mystic rood'. All images are shadows of the object they indicate. They are not shadows in the sense of being the idea in a lesser, imitative actuality. Images are actual shadows of a physical reality. Chesterton examines the process in a review of Eliot's essay on Dante, and goes on to speak of the essential 'irrelevancy' of Dante's images. The distance and dissimilarity that exists between them and the object, makes the object more real by emphasising the impossibility of expressing it. Further, he suggests that many images are needed, none pretending to be the reality, because 'It prevents the *mere* idolatry of one shadow in one mirror, as if it were the origin of all'. Other techniques that he suggests for creating allegorical expression and avoiding direct representation are the old standbys of riddle, metre and rhyme encountered in *Manalive*.

As the great poet wishes to communicate divine truth he must use the modes of the mystic artist, even though he may only incorporate them into his own technique. We noted above that Chesterton felt that the great poet alone was able to put ritual into words. Reality can only be expressed in 'gesture and artistic form'. The great poet achieves the heights of expression when he like the mystic, not only acknowledges the limits of his imagination but incorporates these very limits into a positive mode by indicating God. Chesterton thinks that the height of human creation is to evoke a new image, and images are of their nature things with 'an outline, and therefore a limit'. Great artists like Dante constantly approach the mystic vision in their use of images defined and separate from the reality they indicate. He also notes that 'real imagination gives to an object a sort of ecstatic separation and sanctity' that conveys the divinity of their existence.

However, the poet is also concerned with myth and humanity. Because there may be no absolute standard behind his images they can be vulgarised; they 'stand for strong impressions' only as 'arbitrary and accidental' images. Chesterton looks at this potential debasement of a mode in heraldry. He notes that heraldry began as an art and 'afterwards degenerated into a science'. When it lost its primary function to relate man to his divine meaning, it still possessed the possibility of doing so, of becoming allegorical. But the loss of its mystic intent meant that it became for the most part accidental. Similarly the strength of myth which contains part of man's divinity by virtue of being his ultimate creation, degenerates into the popular and relative form of metaphor. With the 'mental relapse' into metaphor goes the substitute for reason, the cliché; and he recognises that 'in this fall of man's chosen symbols, there may well be a symbol of his own fall'. Yet even here he differentiates between the myth of the great poet and the self-centred propaganda of the fantasist for:

Mythology is simply believing whatever you can imagine. Propaganda is, more often, believing that other people will believe whatever you can invent. [14]

In an essay of 1935,[15] Chesterton finally has the strength to explain what he has been afraid of since the beginning of his artistic career. The author tells us of a book he has not written which was to deal with the substance of dreams. But, rather than the 'nightmares of Freud' which produce 'perilous stuff that weighs upon the heart', he was to have written a pantomime or parable of light nonsense. What he visualised was the solipsist state come true; the dreamer fully able to realise his dreams, the writer actually able to create a reality through metaphor. The intent was to 'suggest how intolerable such imaginative omnipotence would really be. It would be like walking upon ever-sinking and shifting shingle.' He goes on to condemn the modern author for discovering 'in an omnipotence to which he has no claim, an impotence for which he has no cure'. He adds that he himself has made the mistake of using metaphors as empty shells rather than concrete realities and has mislead his readers dangerously.

Despite the fact that initially communication with society was to ensure personal sanity, the converse is true. An essential fault in personal authority and the solipsist vision is that it inhibits communication with a public. Just as we saw that communication with society was the test of the value of the mystic, so it is for the great artist. Where Chesterton most strongly criticises modern art is in its lack of communication. Both mystics and great artists are included in his essentials of artistic expression that lead up to this necessary communication. For him the aesthetic process functions by the principle of contrast because just as exaggeration reveals the real outline of an object, the difference of an image from its reality defines the reality. Similarly, just as the form of exaggeration is unquestionable, so contrast is definite; neither makes pretence to represent the object, and both may then reveal its beauty. The presence of contrast also implies judgement, because one is assessing the relationship of object and image. As the critic points out in an essay on the comic contrast 'Art can be immoral, but cannot be unmoral. Unmoral comedy is rapidly ceasing to be comic', or to be art. All art should have a purpose, a morality. It is not 'mere moralizing' but a fruition, a goal, an answer. Modern art fails because it has no answers, it has nothing to communicate.

Chesterton's most extensive essay on modern art is an essay called 'The Spirit of the Age'.[16] The spirit he perceives in the early twentieth century is one of movement. Neither poetry nor prose can find goals or fruitions; they must be serial not climactic. Just as we have seen him praise Pound and Wyndam Lewis for 'making it new' and condemning them for writing with no hope or aim; so he here praises the individual advances these men make, yet warns that in their 'isolation is a certain irresponsibility about communal ideals'. Elsewhere he notes the immorality of those who attempt a 'soothing and insulated condition of intellect' that avoids all ethical commitment. The poet can only be great if he has a goal and communicates it. He is supreme among men because he 'can say exactly what he means, and that most men cannot'. The critic recalls his words about St Francis and states:

> the other name of Poet is Pontifex; or the Builder of the Bridge. And if there is not a real bridge between his brain and ours, it is useless to argue about whether it broken down at out end or his. He has not got the communication. [17]

Another essay reiterates the example. The poet, like the priest, is a 'builder of the bridge'; his claim is to cross between 'unspoken and seemingly unspeakable truths to the world of spoken words'. But there is no triumph until the bridge is built, the word spoken, and 'above all, when it is heard'.

The criticism of all the major writers of this period and earlier is based on the fact that they are not concerned enough about an absolute standard, an external goal. All are too relative, too individual and cannot communicate. What they have instead is an interpreter, a middleman. Chesterton abhors this phenomenon for two reasons. The first is that an interpreter interferes with the 'awful obstetrics of art'. The poet is encouraged to believe that the poem is finished, is clear and can communicate because a literary sycophant says it is so. Second, the poet comes to depend upon the clique understanding him, rather than explaining himself. This is a negation of the whole poetic process which is to describe the indescribable so that it is accessible to others; it is a throwing away of a responsibility which defines the role of the poet. The poet must include the role of the mystic artist for he must interpret as well as create.

There is another more serious implication arising from the loss of communication. Art with no fruition is an image with no reality. It becomes an idol. The process is implied in a review of a book about the Pre-Raphaelites, whom the critic links directly with the Aesthetes. He says that they tried 'to make a short cut to mystical visions without really believing in mysticism'. They worship the form of medieval art without understanding catholic philosophy. The same accusation is made of the Imagist poets 'those singular idolaters', who gave the reader an image without an idea. Idolatry is the tool of the literary technologist, the fantasist; idolatry is a 'danger to the soul' because it is a 'worship of the instrument'.

The point is that these artists lack what is necessary to communicate: a religious idea. Therefore they make a religion out of their art. True creation is found in poets such as Shakespeare, whose creation of an image reveals 'a moral mystery'. Significantly the image 'is not only a speech, but a gesture'. Similarly in Dante the images 'are not to be worshipped'; there is an idea behind them all before which the poet falls in praise. Chesterton acknowledges that 'every image is an idol' in one sense, and goes on to say that this makes it absolutely necessary that the images be religious. Yet he concludes by stating that if art is great art, in other words if it accepts its responsibility to communicate and does not degenerate into despotism or anarchy, it cannot fail to be religious; therefore its images can never be idols. 'Religion is the sense of ultimate reality' and therefore art which expresses this reality, which assumes a mystic function, is religious. The only codicil he appears to add to this pronouncement is that controversial and unpopular art will be that which expresses a religious idea that is contrary to the fundamental religious belief of the public.

The style that a man uses is seen to be intrinsically part of the truth he is communicating. Significantly, when we turn to *The Everlasting Man*, Chesterton's statement of faith after conversion to Roman Catholicism, we find it conducted on a basis of expressive modes. *Orthodoxy*, the earlier statement of Anglo-Catholic faith, contained much that was relevant to the new positive approach to art and its relation to religion through the concept of the mystic artist. But it was a tentative exploration of an area which was most thoroughly traversed and mapped in the following two decades. In *The Everlasting Man*, published in 1925, Chesterton uses his now sophisticated understanding of expressive modes to examine the nature of his religious belief.

The book is divided into two parts. The first looks at man as a human being; it examines his human modes of expression, principally myth and philosophy. The intent is to demonstrate the inadequacy of human expression in communicating religious meaning, yet to acknowledge its value as a human characteristic. The second part of the book attempts to uncover what religion is for the author, and along the way looks at potential modes for revealing it to others. The book begins by stating that 'Art is the signature of man'. Immediately the limitations of this are pointed out. Man may be 'creator as well as creature', but his creations are reproductions of 'things in shadow or representative shape'. The beginning of the second section notes that God also is an artist, but 'the pictures that he made had come to life'. Chesterton's faith and sanity are firmly based in the belief the God created matter and that man only recreates from it.

Having begun by defining man as an artist, Chesterton proceeds to examine the process of the imagination in fine detail. He starts with the image of the mind as a mirror, which he used in discussing Dante and which is an important part of his personal vocabulary. Again, he does not use the image to mean that man perfectly imitates the external in art. Rather it is a mirror because it can only reflect; yet it is unique for no other animal can even reflect nature. Things can only be seen 'like shining shadows in a vision', but they can be seen. With a mind like a mirror 'Man is the microcosm; . . . man is the image of God'. Chesterton suggests that the power of imagination lies in a suggestion of 'sacramental feelings of the magic in material sub-stances', that myths and metaphors were a way of indicating some kind of 'external soul' necessary to man's existence. As a result images are 'shadows of things seen through the veil'; and work best when quite external to objects they represent. They always suggest something further than what they are themselves.

Myths are the grand works of imagination and poetry. They are definitely to be distinguished from mere diagrams. They should be judged by the guide of aesthetics or 'feelings', because they are not allegories or abstractions. However, they may be 'images almost concentrated into idols' because they are always based on a human authority. Myths may be sincere in expressing the 'real spiritualities' of life; but the sincerity is that of art, it 'is not sincere in the same sense as morality'. Any attempt to worship a myth as a religion becomes the foundation of human tragedy: man worshipping himself and finding himself wanting. Chesterton links this with the fundamental process of imagination, saying the myth as a shadow:

> reproduces shape not texture. These things were something *like* the real thing; and to say that they were like is to say that they were different . . . it is in this sense of identity that a myth is not a man. (117)

Further a poet can be no priest bringing definite external authority; the religion of mythology is of a 'dreamer and idealist' desiring the effects of human authority. As a result, it is open to distortion, it is not absolute.

On this basis Chesterton argues that Christ must not be presented as a myth. He backs up his point by saying the whole point about God is that he was something that primitive peoples knew existed but never spoke about. Human speech and its artistic forms cannot express God because of the inherent function of 'like' in the imagistic process. But further imaginative speech is doubly unsuitable for religious expression because it can be rotted away by rationalism. Myths are fundamentally individual and human; they convey nothing about the unknown. There is always the potential for them to become false, relative stories opposed to the truth of God. At the root they are the impetus of paganism, which is the attempt to reach God by the imagination alone. Religion is a vision received through faith, but it is a vision of reality. Mythology can never be considered as 'real'; it is one step removed from reality; it is only a shadow of reality.

However, the author is at pains to emphasise that if religion is not mythology, neither is it philosophy; and the mythology contributes far more to the expression of religion than does philosophy. Imagination, because of its recognition of the value of material and substance, does at least acknowledge an external. Philosophy tends to make diagrams and patterns out of religion that become totally internalised. Religion is 'not a pattern but a picture', yet one must always remember that it *is* life, not just *like* life. Chesterton also states that in Christianity, philosophy and myth can be combined; the division between them is bridged by the incarnation. Again it is myth's carnality, providing an analogy to the incarnation, that makes it so valuable. But rather than either myth or philosophy explaining Christ, Christ explains them through the incarnation.

In the second part of *The Everlasting Man* Chesterton examines his belief that in order to express the presence of God man must turn to other modes. The author recognises this as a problem but insists on its necessity. He does so by pointing out his understanding of Plato and Aristotle. Plato 'anticipated the Catholic Realism' by insisting that ideas were realities. However, Plato unfortunately seems sometimes to imply that man is unnecessary if he conflicts with ideas. Aristotle went further; he 'anticipated more fully the sacramental sanity' of body and soul. Just as the sacramental unity of idea and image is the basis of imagination, so the sacramental unity of God and word is the basis of religious expression. It is a human affirmation of the incarnation of God. Chesterton begins his examination of religious expression by looking at the allegory of the cross. The cross 'does convey, almost as by a mathematical diagram, the truth about the real point at issue; the idea of a conflict stretching outwards into eternity'. He adds that the cross is only a figure while the truth 'is abstract and absolute; though not very easy to sum up except by such figures'. The author turns for help to the Bible and notes that only in *The Book of Job* does there seem to be an 'early meeting of poetry and philosophy', and this only communicates by providing greater mystery.

The absolute expression of God being impossible, Chesterton turns to the expression of the mystery that indicates his presence. This he finds in the *New Testament* which is itself centred around the mystery of Christ's incarnation, and leaves much 'to be guessed at or explained'. Again the techniques used are gesture, 'enigmatic silence', ironical reply, riddles, and fable. But the most important aspect is the use of a technique which piles 'tower upon tower by the use of the *a fortiori*'. He speaks of the three levels of the parable of the lilies of the field. Christ first notes the smallness and simplicity of a flower; he then suddenly expands its meaning to vast proportions; and just as suddenly shrivels it to nothing. The three degrees indicate a truly 'superior mind' that can compare 'a lower thing with a higher and yet that higher with a higher still' or can think 'on three planes at once'. A similar idea of 'simultaneous happenings on different levels of life' can be found in medieval art and the mystery plays, before the use of realism and perspective that heralded the Renaissance, entered painting and drama.

The use of different degrees of the comparative is the analogical function and is important because in building layers of reality it indicates by implication a supreme reality which is God. Secondly, it admits through its portrayal of different degrees, that it cannot convey any reality totally in one expression. Chesterton allies both these aspects of analogy to the sanity of man. The fact that Christ used analogy shows that he was without 'megalomania'. He indicated his divinity but without the false pride of proclaiming total divinity. Significantly, the author adds that a man who claims to be God must either *be* God or be a madman. Since no one ever suggested that Christ was mad, he must be God. The corollary is that ordinary men who claim to be God *are* mad; and that the only way of avoiding this oneself and yet expressing the divinity of one's humanity, is to use analogy. The one event which eludes even analogy in Chesterton's eyes, is the crucifixion. The possibility that 'God had been forsaken of God', that Christ was mad, that there is no God, is too awful an extremity to convey except by 'a sound that can produce a silence'. The existence of the church is justified in a similar manner. The author suggests that if it had passed away as only another myth, it would have been conveying a myth 'in which the mind struck the sky and broke', for man cannot sustain the experience of being God without going mad. However, it survived; it did not pass away; therefore, it was not conveying a myth about insanity but a reality about God. The church is a messenger which does not dream or argue about the existence of Christianity but 'delivers it as it is'. Its function is to guide the interpretation of the analogies that surround the mystery of God and Christ in the Bible. Because it does this the author says that the Catholic religion is the only thing that has remained stable and sane.

Chesterton's use of analogy throughout his work indicates his own need for stability and sanity. Analogy and the allegorical mode Chesterton uses it in, allow him to avoid the blasphemy of attempting to be God through his art. He recognises his limitations at the same time as indicating his divinity and creative function as a man. The expression itself is essential for it unifies religion and morality with the writer. But further, the author says that self-expression is the only human act that justifies, by analogy, the concept of God's love. Self-expression through analogy is a limitation, a confession of humanity. It is a materalisation and an attempt to link the divine and the human. Its indication of God is a prayer that God will transcend its limitation. Just so God's love is manifested through all these aspects in the analogy of himself, which is Christ.

9 Inner Landscapes: 1900—1935

The three components of religion, morality and expression come together in the one art form in which Chesterton seems completely at home: the detective story. At the heart of the Father Brown stories is the theme of 'mental and moral morbidity' that is mentioned in *Autobiography*, and which initiated and defined much of the subsequent development of religious and artistic ideas. We have seen the concept hinted at in *Orthodoxy*, as the fear which Christianity stopped with external authority, and because of which Chesterton generated his concept of the mystic artist. It was resolved in *The Everlasting Man* by the acceptance of the Catholic faith and the use of analogy in allegory. In the *Autobiography*, Chesterton refers to the meeting with Father O'Connor in 1904 which provided him with an impetus that led to the Father Brown stories. The famous discussion about priests and confessions brought him 'face to face once more with those morbid but vivid problems of the soul' and made him feel that he had 'not found any real spiritual solution of them'. The solution he found in turning to the Catholic church was based on the necessity for accepting external reality because of the existence of an external authority. The Father Brown stories can be seen as exercises by Chesterton as the mystic artist in facing the mental and moral morbidity armed with a sophisticated mode of allegory.

It is perhaps useful to summarise briefly the aspects of Chesterton's idea of the mystic artist in order to recognise the appropriateness of the detective story form. In accepting the Catholic faith the artist accepts an external authority. As a result he not only creates, but because he acknowledges a power beyond him he also interprets. The artist expresses his creative, divine aspect most purely through action and ritual. He exposes his human side in material art which is here allegory. The allegorist is the mystic artist who is also critic or interpreter, performing the essential function of social communication. The critical process not only benefits society, but forces the artist to make an active choice in order to express, and thereby exposes his limitations.

Ritual is enigmatic while allegory attempts to indicate its enigma and present interpretation through analogy, in such forms as fable, parable or detective story. The analogical function of interpretation is through Christian reason, not rationalism or impressionism, philosophy or mythology, which are humanly based systems. The mystic artist is always aware of both ritual and allegory, of acting and communicating and their essential inter-relationship. He is always creative and limited, divine and human, enigmatic and explanatory at the same time. The problem of simultaneously separating yet fusing these aspects is solved in the use of the degrees of analogy which in Christian allegory indicate God, and the divine transcendence of the separation produces sacrament. The process is used in both *The Man Who Was Thursday* and *Manalive* in which the analogical form separated yet fused ritual and allegory within the story through the final indication of God. In both cases the form for the search for meaning and expression is the detective story: in it the central character could employ Christian reason, and experience revelation. Yet the detective story also allows Chesterton to express through allegory the enigma of his own life. He himself uses Christian reason and creates an experience of revelation in order to indicate the transcendent power of God in personal terms.

In turning to the Father Brown stories and the mental and moral morbidity they challenge, one sees that the morbidity is based on the idea of the self as centre, without external authority. The result is either crime if the self-centredness is chosen, or insanity if it is unconsciously fallen into. The role of the detective is to expose the insanity and criminality to reason by being a mystic artist, someone who can identify with the act and find its external meaning. The result of detection for the criminal is confession; and Chesterton's general thesis seems to be that this morbidity can only be faced if there is possibility for confession. The importance of confession is entirely in accord with his own statement that he converted to Roman Catholicism 'To get rid of my sins'. Confession can only exist if God does; and if God exists there can be no self-centredness. Therefore confession becomes a reaffirmation of God. Self-expression in art is a form of confession, for in it one exposes one's limitations. Furthermore, in its need for an audience the art becomes a communication, a praying for the incarnation of divine meaning, for the being of an object to be communicated through the physical medium of art. What we perceive Chesterton expressing as an artist in his own right is the meaning of Christian ritual as he understands it. It is not surprising that while the earlier stories before his conversion stress the function of Christian reason in solving the crime, the later work emphasises its function in saving a man's soul.

The shift in emphasis from solving a crime to saving a soul is paralleled by the essays that Chesterton wrote on the theory of the detective story, yet, as usual, both elements are always partially present. Although the discussion with Father O'Connor occurred in 1904, Chesterton has formed the basis for his ideas as early as 1901 when he contributes six essays to the 'Daily News' on popular literature. Two of these specifically concern detective stories. The first discusses the expression of 'the poetry of modern life' that the detective story uncovers. Chesterton notes that there is no stone or brick 'that is not actually a deliberate symbol, a message from some man', and the detective's job is to interpret the meaning of these objects which are really allegories. Further, he says that the police force is 'romantic' because it attempts to reach a solution and a goal. The order it maintains shows morality as a 'dark and daring' conspiracy. In the second essay the critic is examining the dangers of the form. Even at this early stage of his religious development he says that the ability of the old religions to make the world a mystery by seeking a 'nameless creator' has the 'same kind of immediate and terrified intensity with which the nameless criminal is sought for in a detective story'. However, both processes can mislead by emphasising a false element of success. They encourage one to overvalue the intellectual powers of man that lead to the answer, to worship the man not the divine. What should be the aim of a detective story is revealing 'the heart of things', not showing off human techniques. The critical work on Robert Browning also links detection with religion in *The Ring and the Book*. It states that Browning's poem:

> is of course, essentially speaking, a detective story. Its difference from the ordinary detective story is that it seeks to establish, not the centre of criminal guilt, but the centre of spiritual guilt. (168)

It is important that it is from this observation that he expands his study of Browning's style which eventually starts him on his own journey to the discovery of a mode to express God. It is the concept of spiritual, not criminal guilt that will inform all the detective stories he is to write.

The next extensive essay connects the detective story directly with religious writing. He compares the detective story with religious writings and finds the latter wanting. The 'police novel' reveals the secret all at once, while theological literature tends to let the existence of God 'leak out'. [1] Further detective stories are satisfying because one always knows that 'the great problem will be solved'. In 1930 he again picks up the point with reference to the necessary 'fruition' of a book for 'detective stories . . . must, after all, end by telling us who did it'. [2] The year 1907 also produces the following comment specifically on detective stories:

> The purely imaginative man . . . would perceive the significance of things near to him as clearly as . . . [that] of things far off . . . The best and last word of mysticism is an almost agonizing sense of the preciousness of everything. [3]

This is the first direct linking of the detective to the mystic artist and is contemporaneous with *The Man Who Was Thursday*. Two years later he notes that the detective story writer creates not only a mystery, but also a puzzle. The story must not only be enigmatic but must also indicate a solution. In *Orthodoxy* itself the author speaks of the church as a private detective with the aim of tearing the evil out of man, and of the church pardoning him when he faces his crime. This idea is later developed into the statement that the church created a machinery of pardon in opposition to the state's concentration on punishment: 'It claimed to be a divine detective who helped the criminal to escape by a plea of guilty'. [4] The idea is more fully applied in the function of the court in *Manalive*. Even *The Everlasting Man* contains the reference to priests dressing as priests compared to policemen, 'as if we should be any more free if all the police who shadowed or collared us were plain-clothes detectives'. A further link between the detective and the spiritual story is that in both 'even the moral sympathies may be in doubt'. [5] The fact is a problem for the artist as much as it is for the policeman and the priest, for all have a social duty to carry out as well as an individual.

The same essay that connects the detective with the mystic also speaks of 'a sublime and sacred economy' of their technique. The noticing of minute detail as significant is the basis for the detective method. In 1911 this leads to a distinction between the mystery story and the adventure story. The former deals with detection, is concerned with small things, domestic scenes not large events; while

the latter concentrates on the crime itself. The same distinction is
made in 1929 when the critic notes that adventure stories do not
require the scrutiny of a central event that the detective story does.
After the Great War, when Chesterton begins to stress the moral
rather than the intellectual problems, he begins to take a far greater
interest in the techniques of detective stories. One aspect that is
mentioned is the need for economy, for keeping within the 'classical
unities'. The intensity of the drama depends upon keeping within the
limits of time and place. He continues this thread in an essay of 1922
which stresses the highly technical character of detective stories. The
principles the technique rests on begin with the need for revelation
and surprise. For this to be effective 'the secret should be simple' and
the length should be of a short story. The interest lies not in the
intellectual working out of the crime, but in the meaning it uncovers.
The value of simplicity and compression is high because the story is:

> a drama of masks and not of faces . . . It is a masquerade ball in
> which everybody is disguised . . . until the clock strikes
> twelve . . . we cannot really get at the psychology and phil-
> osophy, the morals and religion, of the thing until we have read the
> last chapter.[6]

The implication is that to continue this 'misunderstanding of fact' too
long, is a dangerous procedure.

The later essays concentrate more on the moral basis and spiritual
core of the detective stories. The year 1925 produces an essay with a
long list of 'DONT'S' for the detective writer.[7] The main points that
emerge are first, that the reader desires to be deceived; and second,
that the character must do the murder, in other words there should be
no extenuating circumstances such as the use of professionals, gangs,
spies and so on. The intent is to avoid any fudging of the moral issue
that murder is a sin. The idea is repeated almost 10 years later in an
essay of 1934. He states that detective stories need criminals and
crime, and must not 'ignore the existence of sin'. Because the plot is
really moral the stories are concerned with conscience and acts of will.
There must never be 'that arbitrary gesture of self ablution and self-
absolution with which some characters in modern stories conclude
the confession of their lives'.[8] The emphasis is on the criminal's act of
choice and the need to expose it. A year later he says that the murderer
should commit his crime for reasons 'immediately, though er-
roneously, satisfactory to his soul and his inner life'. The act of will is

at the root of the distinction between insanity and criminality. He condemns as heresy 'the perpetual itch to describe all crime as lunacy'. [9] The criminal may have lost his innocence but he still has free will. The insane has lost 'more than innocence; he has lost essence'; he has lost the acknowledgement of an external authority. Crime is always a matter of choice, therefore the criminal's soul may always be saved.

While the criticism shows plainly how Chesterton viewed the subject matter and technique of the detective story, it does not touch specifically on the methods of the detective except as he is linked with the mystic. To examine his ideas on method we must go to the detective stories themselves. The first collection of detective stories that Chesterton publishes is *The Club of Queer Trades*. The stories, while all centred on an event, are really concerned with how the mind of the detective, Basil Grant, works. The main plan of the short stories is similar to the Sherlock Holmes story. We have a Watson in the narrator. The action takes place out of a comfortable bachelor apartment in central London, and is nearly always initiated by a sudden arrival on the step of a mystery that needs to be solved. However, the whole intent is to reverse the Sherlock Holmes method of thought. The book is not a parody but a demonstration of a different kind of thinking. The rational is not satirised but merely shown to be ineffective. The author speaks of the 'fantasies of detective deduction' that are worthless in the face of a moral problem.

The first story sets up the lines along which the remainder will run. The narrator is familiar and friendly and appears trustworthy because he seems to expect us to know things about the situation. But once inside the story he is merely matter for Basil Grant to work upon. He provides the 'normal' response, carrying the reader into the event with ordinary eyes. When Basil Grant reveals the truth to him, we also experience it as a revelation. Grant himself is described as a poet, a man who needs people but who can do without them. We are also told that he was a judge who went mad on the bench. In the first case he forms an impression about a story and combines it with common sense and impartial observation. It is impossible for him to explain how he feels, for he has no logic to his actions. He judges the 'spiritual atmosphere' of the case. For him 'facts obscure the truth' so he follows his intuition until he discovers the solution. In contrast is Basil's brother Rupert who is a professional detective. He is rational in the Sherlock Holmes style and insists that 'It's a matter of fact'.

Similarly his client, at the centre of the mystery, is 'incurably sane', rational, 'perfectly clear and intellectual'. But neither Rupert nor his client can solve the mystery. The rational approach limits one's understanding to oneself. Basil Grant succeeds because he combines personal intuition with objective views of the characteristics of the event itself.

The remaining stories each show Basil Grant working out a particular problem in a particular way. All contribute to the sense of looking for the unique in a person, thing or event by insisting on the combination of intuition with common sense observation, objectivity, and knowledge of, but not enslavement to, facts. In each case the narrator thinks that Basil is mad until the event is explained; and this pre-judgement underlines the fact that sanity depends on having reasons for relating objects to meaning. The final story gets to the heart of the mystery of Grant himself. We are told that he functions in this way because he is a moral judge. He explains that he disagreed with the objectives of state law operating 'by a mean rule' of fact. As a result he offered himself as a 'moral judge to settle purely moral differences'. It is important that his powers, which are only briefly seen in action in one story, are only effective if the criminal chooses to observe them; they are not 'coercive' but dependent on 'the honour of the culprits'. While the emphasis of the stories is undoubtedly on solving the crime, they also contain implications which will be developed later. The basic components of a moral judge, the free will of the criminal, and the need for common sense and intuition in reasoning out the answer are all here waiting to take on different proportions.

The Father Brown stories themselves make up five books. Two of them are pre-War, 1911 and 1914; two of them are written during the period 1926-7, and the last in 1935, a year before his death. This last, *The Scandal of Father Brown*, is one of the best examples of Chesterton at his worst and adds little to our understanding of him or his work. The remaining four, however, constitute a fascinating summary of Chesterton practising what he preached. He has stated how struck he was by the idea of a seemingly innocent priest knowing as much as, if not more than, the criminal. All the Father Brown books are essentially studies of the relationship between the two men. The title of the first book is *The Innocence of Father Brown*, and indeed the initial story in it establishes the contrast between the priest's innocence and his vast knowledge of criminality. But rather than weakening the effect of the remaining stories by establishing the contrast so early in the book, it leaves open the possibility of exploring how this innocent mind works.

It is important to recognise that the narrator does not come out and say 'this is how it works'; he does not impose a theory on his character. We are presented with events within which Father Brown thinks and acts, and we understand from these. There appear to be two basic facets of Father Brown's mind: the power of observation, and a knowledge of and sympathy with human nature. The second aspect is different with each human being. In one case the priest solves the murder by realising that most people do not notice men in uniform such as postmen; they are so habitually accepted that no one thinks to take them into account. In another he works from the impossibility of a constantly cheerful human nature. Yet this aspect is ultimately useless without that of observation, and both are necessary to make up Father Brown's process of reasoning.

The function of his mind is outlined with great clarity in the third story 'The Queer Feet'. Father Brown is locked in a room he has never been in before and is listening to the sound of footsteps outside. The priest is first seen with his perceptive senses just awakening to the sound of the footsteps; he then becomes fully conscious of, and attentive to, the sound as he tries to understand the pattern they are making. The narrator describes Father Brown's imagination as a 'kind of vision' interspersed with rational attempts at explanation. The visionary aspect maddens him with a smell of evil and he continually has to conquer it with his rational powers. Just as he sees the man belonging to the steps he suddenly gets an inspiration; he loses his head but 'His head was always most valuable when he had lost it'. All his observations come together to provide the answer. The story is interesting because it emphasises the two aspects of rationalism and impressionism as both being part of an observing imaginative process. Yet it also makes clear that the final answer cannot be achieved except by inspiration of human knowledge. Both are essential to the process of reason.

One of the major concerns of the book is the relation of the detective to the criminal. However, Chesterton first presents us with Father Brown in relation to the average rational detective. In the initial story it is the detective Valentin who is most closely studied, and the climax, while humorous in the contrasts it produces between the priest and the criminal, is more telling in the contrasts between Valentin and Father Brown. Valentin is a 'sceptic' whose intellectual successes have been gained by 'plodding logic'. He was supremely reasonable in the sense of rational, and whenever he encounted irrationality he 'coldly and carefully followed the train of the unreasonable'. Valentin's lack is in failing to distinguish between rational reasoning and other forms; between his own logic and other people's. When he finds the criminal he still does not understand that he has done so. The detective hides in the bushes while Father Brown, and Flambeau, disguised as a priest, discuss reason. Yet because Valentin is so self-oriented in his attitude to reason he cannot recognise the theological mistake Flambeau makes in conjecturing that in other worlds 'reason is utterly unreasonable', and almost goes away empty-handed. Father Brown's reason is really based in a good common sense understanding of people he has known. He can identify with the criminal and spirit away the cross that he wants to steal; but he also prevents the crime by leading Valentin to the spot by a series of conscious mistakes. He is both artist in laying his criminal trail of evidence and critic in interpreting Flambeau's motives. Significantly, it is Valentin who says 'The criminal is the creative artist, the detective only the critic'. Father Brown is the mystic who can combine both functions.

Both kinds of detective agree that the criminal is purely artist. Indeed the narrator himself calls Flambeau an 'artist and a sportsman'. In another story Father Brown says 'A crime . . . is like any other work of art'. Divine or diabolic, the centre of all art is simple; and the priest is able to solve the crime he is examining by piercing through the complicated exterior to this centre. Later on, he briefly distinguishes between crime as artistically valuable and crime as degenerate fantasy. Artistic crime has much in common with a miracle which 'is startling; but it is simple'. The power of miracles comes 'directly from God (or the devil) instead of indirectly from human wills'. While crime always assumes the human will as central, it approaches great art in the measure of external responsibility it acknowledges. Self-centred crime is always complicated and deliberately mystifying in its centre. Flambeau says that when he created a crime he took an artistic care to suit it to the landscape or season in which it was committed. Yet he was not a mystic artist working entirely from externals; he 'always made up the story' himself and carried it out as quickly as possible. The most uncanny story of the book 'The Sins of Prince Saradine' is based on the degeneration of one of Flambeau's original crimes into a 'copy' that makes it an evil travesty of the original. Father Brown points out that the degeneration is inevitable because 'no man had ever been able to keep on one level of evil', and it is this observation which reforms Flambeau.

There is, however, a big difference between Flambeau, the criminal who can say that without positive proof of an external he may as well be the centre of the world, and the man who really thinks he is the centre. The latter type is the madman, and the central example is Valentin himself in the second story 'The Secret Garden'. The reader is given his first clue to the situation when Valentin is described as 'one of the great humanitarian French "Free thinkers"'. In Chesterton's mind this is linked with the Age of Reason, the overthrow of the church and the assumption of the supremacy of man. Valentin was only aware of his own reason. He assumed the right to be God, to judge others coldly. When he committed a crime he did it without artistic inspiration. There was no wish to create something with an admirable centre, only something with disorder. Finally he commits the ultimate crime of suicide, which for Chesterton was terrible in its denial of the value of life, and was a crime against every other man alive. A subsidiary example of the madman is the anglican priest who kills his own brother for committing adultery. The reason he does so is that he sees his brother entering the woman's house as he prays from a high tower of his church. The narrator describes the view as 'the monstrous fore-shortening and disproportion, the dizzy perspectives, the glimpses of great things small and small things great'. Father Brown goes on to add that someone he knew, standing in such a place 'fancied he was God'. It is because of this feeling that the other priest had taken the law into his own hands and killed his brother.

Significantly, almost every story contains an example of the horror of madness that Father Brown experiences before he can apply his reason and understand the criminal. In 'The Queer Feet' part of the process of his observing was the swing into the horror of impressionist flux when no rational answer was apparent. During another case his is sickened by a nightmare of his imagination, only recovering 'his mental health by an emphatic effort'. Just before he solves the case he feels that 'Thought seemed to be something enormous that suddenly slipped out' of his grasp. The mirror as an image of ambiguity occurs in the Saradine story. Here, because the mirrors are all meant to imitate and copy, they become purveyors of distortion that 'torture' the priest. He is 'like a man in a nightmare'; 'Somehow he had not seen the real story, but some game or masque'. The final story speaks of the moment of crisis 'as if all reason had broken up and the universe were turning into a brainless harlequinade'. Father Brown has to personally experience the state of mind that believes it is central before he can go on to interpret the crime.

From this first book Father Brown emerges as the detective exercising Christian reason and as the mystic artist, both creative and interpretative. The purpose of this detection is not only the finding out of the crime, but also, although this is not emphasised, the obtaining of a repentance from the criminal. The narrator presents the priest's mind rather than his character. At the start of each story an atmosphere is created for the situation against which Father Brown works. The oddly thin impression of the character of Father Brown, is due to a presentation of his reasoning rather than his personality. He is viewed mainly as an allegory for the function of the church not as a person. His abrupt departures soon after the crimes are solved stress Chesterton's intention to dwell not on the intellectual powers that reach the solution, but on what the solution itself reveals. Explicitly or implicitly there is certainly a note of extending the meaning beyond the event to the human aspect of the participants.

It is curious that the second pre-War book, *The Wisdom of Father Brown*, tends to dwell mainly on the intellectual aspect of detection. While technically adept, the book is less humane; and the narrator is detached as if manipulating Father Brown almost mechanically. The emphasis on Father Brown's observations rather than on his human knowledge is a progression indicated in the title of the book which has changed from the 'innocence' to the 'wisdom'. There is one specific reference in the first story which casts light on the change. The narrator describes the priest on the verge of finding the solution to a crime. His face was frowning:

> It was not the blank curiosity of his first innocence. It was rather the creative curiosity which comes when a man has the beginnings of an idea.[19]

The 'creative curiosity' of the detective process becomes the subject of the book as Chesterton places Father Brown in opposition to other methods of detection. His role is to interpret correctly the assumptions others make, but not necessarily to apply them to the criminal.

Wisdom is directed towards the perception of truth behind the superficial detail, the mask or appearance of things. However, the aim of the process is also to demonstrate that all the other methods of logic have built-in assumptions that obscure the truth. The initial story deals with rational analysis, the criminologist *versus* Father Brown. It introduces the meticulous detective, organised, 'rigid' and rational. When confronted by the mystery that Father Brown takes him to, he at once says 'it is best to look first to the main tendencies of Nature'. He begins by observing the chaos of the room where the crime was committed and adapting every detail in it to fit his theory. Father Brown realises the truth by waiting to perceive it, allowing the facts to yield their own answer. When he realises the solution he tells the criminologist that he is a poet; his theory is a poem. He has created a crime, 'How much more godlike that is than if you had only ferreted out the mere facts'. The rationalist is limited by the limits of his own reason; he cannot solve the crime because he cannot see it as it is.

A similar example is found in the case of the lie detector *versus* Father Brown. The governor of a United States state has just acquired a lie detector. He is sure that merely because it cannot lie it must therefore tell the truth. But a machine is limited to the man who uses it. It may give an impression of the truth but is dependent on the interpretation of its results. As Father Brown points out, 'How do you know you observed it right?' The use of machines is even more dangerous because the man using them is more open to suggestion since he thinks them factual. Father Brown, with access to exactly the same facts, reads them for what they say, not for what he wants them to say. The detective cannot evade a personal responsibility in his interpretation, he too must choose, not just select.

One major assumption that Father Brown is fighting is that the appearance of a person or object exactly reflects its identity. The fear of the unknown is all too easily achieved if the connection between appearance and identity is not understood because it is not clear. A second theme in the book is that of impressionistic analysis that is based on this mistake. The root of the study of mistaken identity is found in 'The Perishing of the Pendragons'. The reader finds Father Brown on a boat. He is listening to 'trivialities' about the house he is going to while trying to quiet his sea-sickness. A little later we are told that he 'was clever in analyzing his own mystification' and is trying to do so as they approach the house that is their destination. However, he gets more mystified as he gets closer to shore; he grows 'a little fanciful' thinking that he is in a nightmare.

On entering the house the priest and his friends try to interpret the carved symbols over the door but cannot, and his friends begin to feel the fear of superstition. However, over dinner the priest begins to understand. He is being served by two servants in yellow livery and immediately thinks of the word 'canary' although canary birds are not yellow:

> The priest's instinctive trick of analyzing his own impressions told
> him that the colour and the near coat-tails of these bipeds had
> suggested the word Canary. (132)

The explicit recognition of an associative process that obscures the truth is what leads him to recognise that a map which is purported to be of the Pacific is really of the river they sailed down. Knowing this he can interpret the symbols on the door and the trivial tales about the house in the light of the map, and avert a murder. The associative construction of the literary invention was intended to obscure meaning by relying on an unquestioning and careless acceptance of the meaning of the words. But Father Brown's ability to pierce to essence revealed an identity far removed from the superficially accepted one.

The first group of stories examines the over-rational emphasis, and the second the impressionistic emphasis in detection. Father Brown himself concentrates on overcoming the materialist and superstitious errors arising from these assumptions, through the use of common sense. The final story shows him in a personal crusade against a superstition that has arisen around someone being shot in a 'weapon-less' land. Knowing that no country would be without weapons for defense, he works from there to discover that a certain army officer killed the man. He also refuses to be caught by the material fact that there are no weapons and the ensuing superstition about the death. Father Brown's method is to involve both aspects in Christian reason. However, while he has explained the crime itself, he has left unexplained many small details. The situation leads to an interesting structural development: the extension of a second mystery beyond the crime.

The beginnings of the stories in the book are descriptions of scenes and details that provide all the information necessary for the ensuing assumptions. The stories go on to follow through these assumptions, to solve the crime; as such the introductions are appropriate to the emphasis on technique. The endings however are unsatisfactory. They do not let Father Brown just explain and vanish, but the explanations refer to the social and moral problems of a second mystery. Quite often this second mystery seems to be more important than the crime in that it illuminates the meaning and value of the technical solution. But except for 'The Man in the Passage' the second mysteries are difficult to perceive. Further, they often appear to centre around a point of Chesterton's propaganda such as Jews, voodoo, machines and so on, not around purely human moral issues. As a result many of the stories seem weak, with little point; some such as 'The God of the Gongs' are even careless and obtuse. Father Brown appears to be dangerously close to a purely mechanical character employing non-mechanical powers, just so that the author can create fantastic propaganda. It is important to remember that the stories are contemporaneous with *The Flying Inn*. They contain aspects of Chesterton's loss of balance that are also evident in the novel, and probably for the same stressful reasons.

Chesterton does not publish another collection of Father Brown stories until 1926 and *The Incredulity of Father Brown*. The book is probably the best collection of the five. In it the use of a two-part mystery is clear and effective. Father Brown solves each crime and then goes on to deal with the consequential, human problems of those involved. It is interesting in this respect that the only major group of detective stories he writes between 1914 and 1926 is *The Man Who Knew Too Much*. The central protagonist, Horne Fisher, solves all the crimes through a deep understanding of human nature combined with close observation of the situation in question. But Fisher can do no more than solve the crimes. He is the official detective; he cannot save souls. Finally he is effective by dying for others. Apart from Chesterton's propaganda purposes, the stories are used to show the ineffectiveness of merely solving a crime. He now fully accepts the need to portray his detective as going further to save souls.

The Incredulity takes its direction from the initial story. Father Brown is humanised, dealt with as a person relating to other human beings. The solving of the crime is still important because it allows the narrator to show the reasoning process at work, but it is incomplete without the concern for the criminal which follows. As a critic and an artist, the priest must first interpret and then re-express the crime. The functions come to be parallel with solving the crime and helping those involved. In *The Wisdom* he solved the crime by finding a middle way between, yet fusing the material and the spiritual, the rational and the impressionistic sides of the evidence through Christian reason. The process was purely his detective method. Here we have a far more complex situation because we are back to dealing with a relationship between the detective and the criminal. Chesterton is identifying the criminal as someone without this reason, off-balance between the material and the spiritual. The criminal is an artist without the ability to indicate external authority, and without the necessary faculty that follows from an acceptance of the external and knowledge of personal limitation. The priest's role is to be aware of the instability. He provides interpretation that allows for re-expression of the crime in the light of Christian reason, and that subjects the acts to an external authority. The book portrays both the inadequate expression of the criminal that reveals him as such, and Father Brown's re-expression.

The initial story, 'The Resurrection of Father Brown' not only changes the less personal atmosphere of the previous collections but also puts Father Brown in the position of potentially being the criminal himself. It makes necessary self-detection. The story places Father Brown in a South American mission where a journalist discovers him, and creates a mythical figure of him for the United States' press. After many stories, the journalist is faced with the problem of how to kill him off. Later, we find out that the priest, in order to stop the stories agrees 'to die and come to life again like Sherlock Holmes'. As a result of the publicity, the priest is also bombarded with requests for testimonials, and one evening having written a testimonial for a wine-merchant he has an intuition of evil. He goes out to discover the source of his oppression and is attacked and killed.

A young engineer in the village sees the attack and the rest of the story is given through his eyes. The technique is a clever move because the engineer, John Race, although an objective scientist, is sympathetic to the ensuing events. His reaction to Father Brown's revival in the middle of his funeral ceremony is doubly strong because of his supposed objectivity. He felt that he had 'burst out of the world of time and space, and to be living in the impossible'. To his further surprise, the first action of the priest is to telegraph his Bishop to say that no miracle has occurred. After this, Race helps Father Brown home.

The process of self-detection that follows this experience leads Father Brown to the conclusion that the whole event was staged. Someone had wanted to fake a miracle, and then discredit it to expose the Catholic church. The kernel of the story is that these people created a fiction for the priest to work within, a human manufacture of the semblance of life. Father Brown works it out by analysing the things he has said to the journalist about his 'fictional death', and the testimonial about the wine which turns out to have been drugged. When he awoke in the middle of the story, his interpretative faculty told him immediately that it was false. His awareness of an authority that had to be maintained, prevented him from the crime of pretending that he was a miracle. When he realises the extent of the possible evil he thanks God for having saved him. If he had accepted the story, he would have accepted an imposition of human will, he would have been an artist without authority, a criminal. Race points out that it was 'pretty practical psychology' for the people to expect him to do just that. Most men would not have been able to interpret the intent so accurately, or resist breaking the illusion.

Central to the story is the creation of a false expression that Father Brown acts within yet manages to interpret before committing the crime. Similarly the remaining stories all concern the criminal as an artist who uses the wrong mode, and how Father Brown interprets for him. Because the criminal is not a mystic artist he does not create or maintain the duality of Father Brown. The priest is able to solve the crime by recognising that an expression does not have a clearly portrayed truth, and going in search of it. He notes that:

> It's the first effect of not believing in God that you lose your common sense, and can't see things as they are. (70—1)

'The Dagger With Wings' is a close study of the mind of the criminal artist. The case is introduced as one for either 'a doctor, or a policeman, or a priest', and the three aspects of insanity, criminality and evil are closely associated with the criminal artist. Apparently a man was being threatened by his step-brother over a court case, and Father Brown goes to see him to ascertain whether he is just over-anxious or if there might be a real basis for the fear. While he is there the step-brother supposedly appears outside and is shot by the brother. However, Father Brown has been attentively aware of a brief change of light outside the glass door. His mind is:

> set dreaming on certain borderlands of thought, with the first white daybreak before the coming of colour, and all that mystery which is alternately veiled and revealed in the symbol of windows and of doors. (135—6)

The dead body is seen as an allegory to be interpreted. Despite the brilliant surface of the brother's story of the fight Father Brown knows otherwise. The brother is really the step-brother who has already killed the brother before the priest arrived.

Later, when explaining to the police, Father Brown comments that the man 'is a sort of monomaniac'. He is only interested in one crime and in doing it supremely well. Such a man is an artist with no social responsibility, and the priest continues by saying that:

> this man had in him a very noble power to be perverted; the power of telling stories. He was a great novelist; only he had twisted his fictive power to practical and to evil ends; to deceiving men with false fact instead of true fiction. (142)

Because he is an artist 'the mask must be to some extent moulded on the face'; he has to express himself at least partially. It is in the discussion of the philosophy that he establishes for his fictional character that he gives himself away. The criminal believes that men are shadows of one reality, that at the centre 'men melt into Man and Man into God'. His misinterpretation of religion as spiritual only, of man as different only in degree from God, indicated the basis of human authority which governed his life and his story. Through this discussion the priest is alerted to the falsity of the tale, and recognises the truth of the body's allegory. Having placed the demoniac magician under police authority, Father Brown goes home; and the description echoes the concern for his youthful fears in the other books of 1926 and 1927 when they mention that 'some forgotten muddle and morbidity seemed to be left behind'.

In virtually every mystery what Father Brown is interpreting is a material medium of expression. The medium is usually verbal, as with his own words in the first story. We have seen him interpreting the analogy of the dead body. One situation calls for the interpretation of a painting, one for the recognition of the 'literary' quality of a man's supposedly spontaneous speech. Each mode leaves something lacking to which Father Brown is sensitive, and when he identifies it he can solve the murder. The next stage is to re-express the act in terms of authority in order to show the criminal the falsity of his belief in human will. In two cases he gets a confession from the criminal by exposing him to the true basis of his act. The case of the monomaniac makes the verbal confession useless since he really believes that he has a right to kill. One confession is even set up as a lie, which will be found out later. Two events are left without resolution, one of which is an unaverted suicide. But the re-expression is necessary not only for the criminal but also for all those with whom he comes in contact. The self-centred perspective perpetrated by the criminal must be corrected so that it does not influence others.

Connected to Father Brown's idea of helping those people around the criminal is his interest in sources of criminality which are not overt. The idea is found in the 'media' programme of his own potential crime. If he had committed it he would have been a criminal, but so would the journalist and wine-merchant indirectly associated with the event. At one point he presents the facts of a case to an unofficial tribunal seeking the murderer of a friend. Father Brown tells them that this man had been killed and they condone the action. Yet when he reveals that the 'murderer' they sought was really the friend, and that someone else had killed the friend, they change their minds. Father Brown then condemns them. He says that their lawlessness in initially condoning the crime invalidates their new call for adherence to the law. The lawlessness was a result of personal desire and unless they were willing to forgo it for a standard of judgement in the law, they had no right to turn to authority afterwards.

Other stories are concerned with this aspect but in one this theme is central. 'The Curse of the Golden Cross' contains the fundamental background to the view of man's potential criminality; it also introduces for the first time the theme of conversion to Christianity as the only solid reform and safeguard. An archaeologist named Smaill has discovered a gold cross with a fish on it. It is important because the design is realistic rather than merely diagrammatic. In the cave where it was found he also saw the fish carved on the wall, but he could not analyze or understand its meaning. The case revolves around someone wanting to kill him because he owns the fish. The murderer sets up a scene based on a superstition, and the fact that it comes true is Father Brown's hint as to the perpetrator. However, when the priest returns to the scene of the crime the murderer has gone. The criminal is a 'monomaniac' with only one aim in mind: to kill Smaill. Thinking that he has done so, he leaves. There will be no confession for him since, as Smaill himself observes he is a 'madman', incapable of accepting any external responsibility.

The real criminal of the story is Smaill himself. Before the actual attack on his life, he is guilty of assuming an unfounded greatness in walking into the trap that the lunatic had prepared for him. Not only does he do this but also he leads others in as well by virtue of their interest in him. Instead of turning to fact he allows the fiction of his greatness to exist. While he recovers from the near-fatal blow he receives, his constant companion is Father Brown. To him he recounts the strange 'Byzantine patterns' of his dreams that continually faded away before the picture of the fish in the cave. Through the priest, he comes to see 'a meaning in the picture'; he comes to understand the analogy that it is making. He realises that the early Christians, the painters of the picture, were persecuted as he was being persecuted. Moreover, they had all civilisation against them and were being persecuted for a faith. In the face of such valid suffering he learns humility, comes to realises his limits, confesses his humanity and implicitly accepts Christianity.

In this collection Father Brown is a man relating to those of who are off balance and without authority. As a mystic artist he has to interpret the words and actions of their crimes and help them re-express them in confession. He has to teach them to be mystic artists for themselves. They must be not only creative but also interpretative. In other words he has to provide them with the authority that puts their personal will in a moral and religious perspective, and prevents insanity, crime and sin. The book is valuable for its own balance. The variety of cases, each with a different emphasis, portrays Father Brown's reacting differently to the human beings in each one. The maturity of the author is reflected in his ability to develop the priest's character as an essential basis for the complex interaction between character and event. The reader perceives in him not only an analogy for the Church and the law, but also a human being trying to come to terms with the potential sin in himself.

In the following year, 1927, *The Secret of Father Brown* was published. Many of the concepts are the same, but they attain an even greater subtlety as Chesterton explores further aspects of the problem. The personal involvement implied in the first story of *The Incredulity* is made explicit in *The Secret*. The actions of Father Brown are not only made clear, but the artistic process of how he carries them out is also examined. The fact is important because it allows the reader to contrast the priest's process with that of the criminal.

The book is organised with a framework of prologue and epilogue within which Chesterton as the author takes great care to express his own meaning. First, the images that the framework contains generate the stories in the rest of the book. But, more than this, the prologue deals with his fundamental method of analogy. The study of it here illuminates the stories which follow in their concentration on the process of expression in both criminal and detective forms. Unfortunately, the framework is not an organic part of the book. While it certainly adds depth to the stories, it is an intellectual activity on the

reader's part. As a result, the stories themselves, although interesting
for their examination of the process, are mechanical in the centre.
They become primarily valuable for their development of concepts
rather than as literary short story efforts.

The actual organisation of Father Brown's method is laboriously
presented, but the study of expression and interpretation is certainly
interesting. In the prologue the reader finds an American asking
Father Brown how he solves his crimes. The priest answers by saying
'it was I who killed all those people'. A startled American tries to turn
the statement into 'a figure of speech', but Father Brown will have
none of it; he denies that he entered only into a superficial
identification and explains in more depth. Just as Chesterton himself
distrusted expression through words because of the potential distortion, so Father Brown says:

> I don't mean just a figure of speech . . . What's the good of
> words . . .? If you try to talk about a truth that's merely moral
> people always think it's merely metaphorical (12)

The priest literally gets 'inside a murderer, thinking his thoughts,
wrestling with the passions . . . Till I am really a murderer'. Significantly he calls the process 'a religious exercise', and indeed it is a ritual
act of total surrender of personal identity to the object he wishes to
understand. It is the action of the purely creative artist.

Then, however, the narrator describes Father Brown's reflections
on 'that introspective style'. The priest looks into his glass of wine
'like the glorious blood-red glass of a martyr's window'. The cup
becomes an analogy for 'the blood of all men' with Father Brown
plunging into it with the necessary 'inverted imagination' of the
criminal. The wine becomes the physical means through which he
reaches the reality of all these experiences. It is 'like a vast red sunset',
'red lanterns', 'a great rose of red crystal' and 'a flame of wild red
beard'. The process of analogical identification brings the experiences
to the man's mind and they begin 'to form themselves into anecdotes
and arguments'. Not only does the description indicate the analogical
process of Father Brown's mind that results in the restricted modes of
anecdote and argument, but also it indicates Chesterton's own
meaning. The overriding analogy of the cup of wine for the
analogical process itself links it with the communion sacrament of the
Church. Analogy is the mode by which a sacramental act of

incarnation can transform the ritual of identification with the criminal into the expression of the act.

The author tells the Father Brown stories through a complex allegorical mode, but Father Brown himself communicates with great difficulty. Indeed his attempts to express himself are often so literal that others misinterpret them. The main factor in his speech is that he is not metaphorical. He provides his solutions by being absolutely literal, by speaking 'in parables', using paradox, or straightforward analogy. Only in the final story does he explain himself directly, and that only after attempting to divert the explanation with an enigmatic analogy. In fact *The Scandal of Father Brown*, in so far as it can contribute anything further to our understanding of Chesterton, does so through its heavier emphasis on the inadequate nature of Father Brown's communication. He knows that he cannot express absolute truth; that he attempts to express anything is evidence of his humility. The uses of parable, paradox, analogy and anecdote are all intentionally inadequate because he has to admit his human limits to indicate the truth.

As usual all the criminals are artists of one kind or another, but here we find an expansion of the idea of a Flambeau-type great criminal as opposed to a degenerate fantasist. 'The Man With Two Beards' is solely concerned with differentiating between a reformed great criminal and a petty criminal. Michael Moonshine is the former. He had an exact artistic sense of balance in how far he would go. By contrast, the criminal of this story has no aesthetic sense. He killed in order to use the body as a stage property and 'all sorts of fantastic finishing touches followed quite naturally from the primary fact'. He was so self-centred that the value of human life was purely in what it could yield him personally. Many of the stories compare the two types of criminal. In one a thief 'a very fine artist in crime' is contrasted with an egoistical actress who murders anyone in her way. Another compares a degenerate self-centred 'artist in revenge' with a murderer committing in crime in 'self-defence'. The final story contrasts the totally controlled artist with the man who is trained to act just well enough to commit a murder and then breaks down.

The self-centred artists each try to create an impression to supplant reality. They are fantasists who do not want their crime to be discovered. They run away from the truth of their crime, or try to construct a facade that obscures it. The horror of crime comes from the obscurity that is created; and Father Brown's role is to delve below the facade, the mask, or the distortion to reveal truth and destroy fear. The other type of criminal, however, is willing to acknowledge the crime; he is penitent, confesses his sin, and often reforms. The implication is that great criminals know that they lack interpretation and almost seek the law or religion as an audience. They would jeopardise their own lives to have their crime examined as a work of art. They create it for itself, not for their own satisfaction as an artist. The epilogue of the book bears out this implication in the analysis Father Brown makes of the anarchist poet. He says that when he identified with this man he realised that he couldn't commit a murder or suicide '*because* he wrote songs of violence. A man who can express himself in song need not express himself in suicide.' He has an audience for this thought in the event of his songs, he does not need to create a crime to express himself.

The point about the criminals is that they all in differing degrees, take their art to be final, to be a reality. Father Brown has to show them that it is not. When he succeeds in exposing the actuality to the criminal they have no recourse but to admit that their art shows their humanity and imperfection. They then need him to re-express themselves in confession. Whereas the law often imposes penance without the criminal truly confessing, with Father Brown there is always the possibility of true confession, penance and pardon. Here the last story is significant. The people involved show themselves ready to condone one crime but condemn another. As with the previous examples of such as situation, Father Brown accuses them of having no absolute standard and therefore no right to appeal to one. They reply that 'There's a limit to human charity', and the priest answers by saying that only Christianity and Christian charity can overcome that limit. The law only forgives criminals who commit 'conventions', only the church can forgive those 'who do things really indefensible'. He then goes on explicitly to say that this is his role as a priest: To give the strength to confess, and then to pardon.

To summarise the ideas that have evolved over Chesterton's 30 years of detective stories, we find the figure of the madman, the criminal and the priest. For the madman his actions are complete and absolute. He lies outside the social sphere for believes that he is the centre and source of the world. Being God, he has no external authority, he needs no audience, no necessary explanation and no confession. The 'mental and moral morbidity' of life arises from the knowledge of this potential insanity. But the fear itself indicates that one is not mad, and here we pass to the figure of the criminal. The criminal act is also intended to be complete and absolute but the criminal always knows the potential limits of the crime. He sins by consciously assuming supreme human authority. Morally the act is evil because it has no social responsibility; it is entirely personal. Similarly as art the crime is wrong because it is created by a distortion of the object or event by personal will.

The criminal either avoids acknowledging the limits or subconsciouly seeks an audience. The latter search is a realisation of the existence of some external authority that is either law or religion. As pointed out, law is seen to be unsatisfactory because it mechanically imposes punishment. Religion provides confession which acknowledges God and the limits of man, thereby exposing the object as it really is and showing the social injustice of the personal view. The acceptance of Christian reason in confession provides the interpretive side to the creation and produces a balanced artist. It is significant that the epilogue of *The Secret* portrays a reformed Flambeau who is a balanced human being. He no longer needs the audience of half the police in the world to admire his crimes, and only with hesitation and reluctance does he admit to the American who he is.

The third figure of the stories is, of course, the priest. His role is to become one with the criminal, to commit the act through ritual identification. Because he is the source of Christian reason he must not only interpret the crime but re-express it in terms of human limitation. Again if we turn to the epilogue of *The Secret* we see that this expression is his own confession. Father Brown is terrified of the possibility of his own sin. He says to the American 'You may think a crime horrible because you could never commit it. I think it horrible because I could commit it'. He acts as a detective not only because of the moral effect on the criminal but also because of his own potential for evil. Through the sacrament of confession, the act and its expression can be transcended by the pardon of God. But the priest is not only identified with the criminal; he is a human being in his own right. As such, Father Brown is a mystic artist whose own detective experiences must be expressed, and this he effects through the limited analogical forms of anecdote and parable. The telling of his story becomes an analogy of the sacrament of communion, which communicates the divine to the human through the incarnation.

What Father Brown becomes is Chesterton's idea of the function of Christian reason in life and the role of the Christian mystic artist. The use of Christian reason reduces the possibility of self-centred acts. It prevents madness and stops evil. The Christian mystic artist has a responsibility to show how Christian reason may be employed, to teach those without it. If they cannot themselves interpret and create he must do it for them. While Father Brown and the process of his mystic reason and expression is the main level of the story, it also clearly functions on the allegorical levels of morality and belief. The detective story as Chesterton creates it gives one a picture with all the necessary evidence. It is an allegory of life in which man has to realise and act upon the significance of the clues he has been given. The author tells us that this is impossible without Christian reason, and the stories become an allegory of the function of Christian ritual in life. Both Chesterton and the priest, as mystic artists with an identifying analogical process, are constantly aware of potential sin; and their expression is a confession of that potential. Not only Father Brown's anecdotes but also Chesterton's life and work function as an analogy for the sacrament of confession.

The Father Brown stories constitute both an interpretation and an expression of Chesterton's philosophy. The *Autobiography* makes the connection explicit when, in its closing pages the author speaks of his life as 'a romance and very much a mystery story'. He says that the journey of his life has brought him the ability to accept the existence of sin as something for which to be grateful, the knowledge that gratitude can only be reached by facing 'the reality about oneself'. Chesterton sums up his life saying:

> my morbidities were mental as well as moral; and sounded the most appalling depths of fundamental scepticism and solipsism. And there again I found that the Church had gone before me and established her adamantine foundations; that she had affirmed the actuality of external things; so that even a madman might hear her voice; and by a revelation in their very brain begin to believe their eyes. (341)

And concludes with:

> This story, therefore can only end as any detective story should end, with its own particular questions answered and its own primary problems solved. (342)

Chesterton's life is a romance and a mystery expressed through the analogy of a detective story. Just as Father Brown's. telling of his experiences becomes an analogy for the sacrament of communion, so

Chesterton's stories become a sacrament of communion between himself and his reader, in which he conveys the existence of the transcending power of God.

10 Survey: 1925—1935

All his life Chesterton felt that he was surrounded by a humanist world. From the early excerpt on Christian Socialism in Maisie Ward's biography, to the extensive essay 'Is Humanism a Religion?' in 1929, he indicates a serious concern with the dangers of human authority. The absolute human creativity implicit for him in the art and philosophy of the nineties split into the twin evils of the aesthetes with their hedonism and pessimism and the didactic rationalists with their Nietzschean superman. These ideas were constantly about during his youth, all insisting on a solipsist view and potential insanity. However, by 1925 the problem they posed did not exist for him personally. In the 1925 foreword to the dramatised version of *The Man Who Was Thursday* he notes:

> I can remember the time when pessimism was dogmatic, when it was even orthodox. The people who had read Schopenhauer regarded themselves as having found out everything and found that it was nothing. Their system was a system and therefore has a character of surrounding the mind. It therefore really resembled a nightmare, in the sense of being imprisoned . . . of being none the less captive because it was rather in a lunatic asylum than a reasonable hell or place of punishment. (4)

He continues by saying that the world in 1925 is different; it may even be breaking up, but the destruction may let in some fresh air.

The result of his trying to counteract the fundamental fear in his life initiated him on his peculiarly individual artistic journey. Yet so extensive were his explorations of the problems of his times that he gathered into his wide vision many of the hopes, fears and partial resolutions of his generation. Chesterton's primary concerns were to express belief in an external and to assert the unity of his inspiration, life and art. As he searched for a mode in which to do so, he denied any permanent value in impressionism and rationalism turning instead to ritual and allegory. In the process his three basic terms

became religion, morality and expression. The last word is significant
for it defines the role of the mystic artist. The mystic artist must relate
the divine to the human, the spiritual to the material. His is not the
role of the saint, the pure man with expression in life; nor is it that of
the great poet with his mythological imagination. Later Chesterton
adds that the role is also different from the philosopher communicating through discursive rationalism. He is trying to find a mode
between discursive and symbolic writing and turns to the use of
allegory. Simultaneously he becomes aware of the mode of fantasy
with its human inventiveness. To avoid its dangers he develops the
analogical function of allegory to indicate the presence of God. As the
style is sophisticated it becomes his own unique form of the detective
story: an expression analogous to, and indicating the existence of,
God's love.

The author insists that he is not an artist. His role is to communicate
the divine; as such he is a mystic with an artistic function. He notes
that the detective story is not great art, and also says that his novels
were:

> not only not as good as a real novelist would have made them, but
> they were not as good as I might have made them myself, if I had
> really even been trying to be a real novelist. [1]

In 1932 he writes his last major work of literary criticism, *Chaucer*. In
this analysis of a great author Chesterton finds all the things he would
have wanted to be if he had not been in the position of more fully
sensing the dangers of humanism. Chaucer's work is tinged with the
colours of humanism, but Chesterton argues that the writer's
Catholic background provided a resilient safeguard against the
dangers inherent in humanism. He is seen as a great poet for he can
'measure the broken strength we call the weakness of man', without
himself being weak. To understand his ability to do so Chesterton
refers us to Chaucer's Roman Catholicism. Like all great poets
Chaucer 'was concerned with things' yet his unique perception of
their value was based on his awareness of the actuality 'of existence, of
the fact that things truly are'. The recognition of existence is
fundamentally religious and calls forth 'a subconscious substance of
gratitude' to God. Chaucer's religion allowed him to accept the
overwhelming intensity of life as a glimpse of God's world and
communicate both its humanity and divinity in his art.

Chesterton bases his study of Chaucer on the recognition of both medieval and modern elements in his style. Both aspects are found to be valuable because Chaucer, being a Catholic, can use either without danger. On the medieval side we find Chesterton picking out points of style that he himself has used. There is the use of heraldry which conveys identity upon everything in Chaucer's work, and fulfils an aspect of his mystic function. There is also his use of decoration which was like a dance, standing for order. The critic states that by 'sheer moral imagination' Chaucer turned the patterns in his work into portraits with concentration on the individual. In doing so he demonstrated the difference:

> between an objective religion, worshipped as an object by the whole people, and a subjective religion studied as a subject only by the religious. (181)

The individual portrait and the subjective religion are the aspects of a modern world which make novels possible. Further, the nineteenth century is seen as the true home of the novel for during that time 'liberal enlightenment' seemed to make the study of individuality not only possible but appropriate.

In Chaucer's time, however, humanism was only just beginning to surface. Chesterton connects an 'irrational humour' in the poet's work with the sixteenth century nonsense of Shakespeare. But whereas Shakespeare's 'wild fantasticality' often breaks the bounds of reason and produces mad characters, Chaucer was still too much of a medieval to 'indulge a fantasy at the expense of everything else'; he was too aware of the order of the world. The whole Renaissance break with medieval tradition is seen as a search for truth at the edges of the human imagination, and that Chaucer had certainly no inclinations towards such a search. The poet is seen as the embodiment of a deep rich turning point in history, religion, and literature; a man able to live in and use the best aspects of both worlds.

Chesterton's sensitivity to the issues involved can be most clearly appreciated in his images for different artistic approaches. We have already noted the use of the mirror and the shadow as the process of myth and symbol in *The Everlasting Man*. Just as myth can be of an ambivalent nature, so the image is ambiguous. In *The New Jerusalem* he speaks of the imaginative properties of the moon which is a 'silver mirror for poets and a most fatal magnet for lunatics'. The positive function of the mirror appears in the statement that the relationship of St Francis to Christ was one of a 'mirror' not a 'light'. The human imagination is only a partial reflection of the world, not divine light shining on it. In the Father Brown stories mirrors are often definitely negative as in their distorting effect in 'The Sins of Prince Saradine'. A very early poem indicates this negative aspects in 'The Mirror of Madmen', an early expression of a solipsistic state. The negative effects are summed up in an essay on modern intellectual mystics. Chesterton states that when this kind of man said he thought a post in the ground wonderful, he meant that it was so not in its own existence but 'inside, in the mirror of his mind'. Since the mystic's mind was entirely made of mirrors:

> glass repeated glass like doors opening inwards for ever, till one could hardly see that inmost chamber of unreality where the post made its last appearance. And as the mirrors of the modern mystic's mind are most of them curved . . . the post in its ultimate reflection looked like all sorts of things . . .[2]

The critic concludes that even though 'they were better poets than I', they only imagined the post; he saw it as it was, wonderful for its material substance. The point about the ambivalent nature of the mirror image is that it is linked to the human imagination. As a result it expresses both the heights and depths of the facets of human communication.

Chesterton also uses the image of the window, specifically the stained glass window, in relation to the function of analogy. We find both the image for human imagination and analogy combined in the introduction to Chaucer's style in the novel, in other words in his modern work. In turning the patterns of the *Decameron* into the portraits of *The Canterbury Tales* Chaucer is the poet as creator of a world, even if only an unreal world. Chesterton goes on to single out two stories, 'Sir Thopas' and 'Chanticler' as important insights by Chaucer into his own method. Both are mockeries of great poets for 'the best in this kind are but shadows'. In 'Sir Thopas' the poet has recreated 'the mystery of the relation of the maker with the thing made'; he has shown that no created object is more than a shadow of its creator. In doing so he has established the basic analogy of God being to man what man is to art. However in both these stories there is a mystical power. Both have:

> the quality by which a very great artist sometimes allows his art to become semi-transparent, and a light to shine through the shadow

pantomine which makes it confess itself a shadowy thing. (26)

Although Chaucer fully explores the human imagination, when he finally comes to assess its value he sees it as nothing before the divine light of God.

In an explanation of Chaucer's invention of the novel form, it is interesting that the process Chesterton observes is identical with that of C. S. Lewis in *The Discarded Image* and Marshall McLuhan in *Through the Vanishing Point*. Chesterton notes that the novel reverses the basic logic of storytelling; 'the story-tellers do not merely exist to tell the stories; the stories exist to tell us something about the story tellers'. Lewis describes the medieval to modern transition as one from the telling 'for the sake of the tale', to telling 'valued only as an opportunity for the lavish and highly individual treatment'. Lewis also contrasts the medieval who will 'feel like looking *in*' a picture, with the modern who 'feels he is looking *out*'.[3] Marshall McLuhan picks up this observation to develop his own definition of the difference. He notes that medieval man is without perspective; he is merely the spectator observing a picture. On the other hand, in creating perspective Renaissance man placed the focus on the audience's point of view so that it appears that he is looking out from himself to a reality in a painting. McLuhan adds that this puts the audience in a passive position because he has to share the painter's perspective, and that this makes influence over other people's sight possible.[4]

McLuhan follows his image right up to the 1900s. At this time he says that Seurat's pointillism created a sense of light behind the dots that made them cast a shadow directly onto the eye of the beholder. From this he notes that it is but one step to the re-introduction of interest in stained glass windows where the light shines through onto the observer. But it is important to differentiate this from Chesterton's stained glass window. His has no point of view at all. An observer watches the light illuminate the world and also himself, but there is no focus.

An extensive exploration of the stained glass window image is found in *The Return of Don Quixote*, another book from the amazingly productive years of 1926 and 1927. A whole moral revolution is expressed through the contrasting techniques of illumination and transparency. Medieval illumination however marvellous, was man working to his artistic best by himself. It 'is in its nature opaque' and must not be confused with the transparency of glass. The final revelation of the novel occurs when a character realises that stained glass windows have to be seen from the inside; 'Inside there was light and outside there was only lead' and this leads to her conversion to Catholicism. It is important here to note a third image, that of the lamp shining on things, which is connected to human authority alone, and to the pagan artist. An article on Thomas Hardy's work observes that there is in the work:

> as in all work really belonging to a pagan world, this character: that all the light is shining on things and not through them. It is all the difference between the gaiety of an old pagan painting or mosaic and the burning clarity of a medieval window. [5]

Here the lamp is an image expressing purely human origin for artistic inspiration and creativity; it ultimately implies that things do not even exist unless man chooses to notice them.

When the conclusion to *Chaucer* is reached it is not surprising that the medieval artistic connections are expressed in the following way: Chesterton states that medievalism contains both mystical faith and pagan vision, and 'for a medieval man, his Paganism was like a wall and his Catholicism was like a window'. Chaucer's own light painted the walls very bright, but 'contrasted with the window, they were still dark'. Indeed it would never cross the mind of any medieval artist that 'the lightness of his mural decoration could approach anywhere near to the light of heaven'. The confession of inadequacy that this contains provides Chesterton with his explanation for Chaucer's 'rejection' of his work. However, the duality of the window and the wall, the stained glass and the lamp, also provides the critic with a basis for understanding the analogies, the thinking on different levels in Chaucer's work. Chesterton notes the influence of analogical thinking in Chaucer's religion, morality and art, and presents it as a stabilising influence of mystic art, linked to Thomist philosophy. The poet had the positive rationalism of Aristotle, the imaginative and pictorial Dante, but above all the mystical and moral St Thomas. These are of course the fundamental elements in Chesterton's own life. He takes most of his philosophical ideas from a personal interpretation of Aristotle; his supreme poet is Dante; and finally the transcending faith of his life that stabilises the rationalism and impressionism, is virtually identical with Thomist belief.

The conclusion of *Chaucer* is that the poet was able to combine the human aspects of communication with those of the mystic artist because he was grounded in solid Roman Catholic tradition.

Chesterton himself spent most of his life moving towards Catholicism. Significantly, only after his conversion does he seem able to appreciate the modern tradition of painters and writers that surround him. Only after 1925 when he is sufficiently confident of his own solution to the problems of his life, does he recognise similar problems in others. The root of Chesterton's concern is in 'human authority' and its growth since the Renaissance resulting in a belief in absolute human communication. What is fascinating about his analysis is the number of searches by widely differing artists, that cross and follow his own explorations.

We have already looked at the Imagist movement with Hulme's rejection of Renaissance humanism and representational art. Earlier still the influential French poet Mallarmé provides a veritable résumé of Chesterton's concerns, with one major difference which emphasises the ambivalent nature of the imagination. With regard to the medium of literature he agrees that description is useless to convey identity. Rather it needs:

> evocation, *allusion, suggestion*. These somewhat arbitrary terms reveal what may well be a very decisive tendency in modern literature, a tendency that limits literature yet sets it free.[6]

The suggestiveness of the technique 'shuns the materials in nature' for literature cannot imitate. Mallarmé is also concerned with the analogical communication of the mystic artist and notes in *Le Livre*:

> Man charged with divine vision has no other mode of expression save the parallelism of pages as a means of expressing the links, the whims, the limpidity on which he gazes.[7]

Creativity is to reveal the existence of objects. McLuhan notes that Mallarmé totally effaces himself because he thinks that the artist's job is 'not to sign but to read signatures. Existence must speak for itself'. However, Mallarmé also thinks of the divine vision as one which he can create. Jacques Maritain notes Mallarmé's letter to Henri Cazalis in which he describes his preparation for writing as a struggle with and destruction of God. Significantly this gives him an 'experience of the void' of nothingness, even a 'faint hope in magic'.[8] Mallarmé not only summarises Chesterton's concerns but also provides an excellent example of the case with which his techniques could, as has been noted with the surrealists, adapt themselves to a diametrically opposed philosophy. The ease with which this occurs can only reinforce the appropriateness to Chesterton of his choice of religious ritual to prevent such distortion.

It should not be forgotten that Chesterton was a painter manqué, and an illustrator all his life. Perhaps because of this talent his writing reflects many of the concerns of modern painters. The medium of painting, probably because it has to deal directly with physical matter, led many twentieth century painters to discuss the aspects of limitation. Picasso for example denies the possibility of art recreating actuality. Klee repeats this, adding that man deforms nature in his attempts to imitate it. Hans Arp develops the concept further, saying that Humanism taught men to believe that they could recreate nature exactly and 'consecrated man to megalomania'. The English champion of the new artists, Roger Fry, goes back to the thirteenth century origins of the Renaissance to explain what he sees as the misguided attempt to imitate. He says the modern artist is not aiming at actuality, but at an equivalent or analogy for life, and that is the only reality possible to him. All these aspects are echoes of the rather neglected Oscar Wilde. A late essay by Fry also reaches agreement with Wilde on the inexplicable and mystic nature of aesthetic response.

It is the similar concern among writers, of the verbal impossibility of absolute communication, that leads many of them to discuss the inadequacies of purely discursive and purely symbolic language. The growing use of allusion, of disjointed and juxtaposed images that is so effectively developed in the poetry of T. S. Eliot is indicative of a common trend among other poets and critics. One of the central factors of Pound's critical directions was the concentration 'on the creative, not upon the mimetic or representational'. J. Middleton Murry also reacting against rational logic and the concept of imitation notes that the artist's ability is to be able to perceive the mystery of an object, that this is 'the pure creative and religious activity of man', and that it is 'sacramental' in recognising not only the thing but also the divine in it. But it is Auden who puts his finger directly on the power and weakness of literature when he states that:

> The notion of writing poetry cannot occur to him [a child], of course, until he has realized that names and things are not identical and that there cannot be an intelligible sacred language.[9]

Chesterton spends most of his life trying to find an approach to a sacred language.

Not surprisingly, where Chesterton's critical theories are most fully reflected is in the work of writers and artists of the same religious persuasion. In many ways Chesterton's often disconnected explorations and discoveries find themselves collected into a coherent whole by the early work of Jacques Maritain. Indeed Maritain's progress from atheism to agnosticism to Bergsonism to Roman Catholicism is not unlike Chesterton's own life. Maritain's *The Philosophy of Art* was translated in 1925 by Father John O'Connor and published at Ditchling, the experimental community with which Chesterton was involved for a time in the mid twenties. In it the writer begins by distinguishing between 'doing' as the domain of morality, and 'making' as the domain of art, but he goes on to say that because an artist labours he cannot help bringing morality to art. Chesterton has always made the same distinction between the two, yet with his conviction of unity between religion, morality and expression, also insists upon their conflation.

Maritain points out that the artist cannot ask for religious fulfilment from art. If he does so, he will go mad, and he cites Rimbaud as an example. The fault lies in taking art and the beauty of it as a final goal, which makes the artist 'an idolator pure and simple'. Art cannot be reality; and 'the art creator is he who finds a *new analogue* of the beautiful'. Again the Renaissance is accused of originating the desire to pretend to the possibility of absolute creation, and this possibility generates the idea that perfect imitation is a false aim of art. Maritain views art as a 'way of letting the clarity of the form shine out upon the material'. Therefore creation is not *ex nihilo*: the artist recreates from material created by God.

Whereas Maritain was interested primarily in philosophy, an explicit echo of Chesterton's concern for language itself can be found in a man of a younger generation: David Jones. Jones also begins by making *ars* and *prudentia* as being indissolubly linked by the action of man's free-will which chooses to create.[10] He agrees that art is religious because it deals with realities and 'the real is sacred and religious', but also that art is not religion. To be able to communicate the religious an artist needs sacrament as an incarnation of external meaning. Pursuing the topic, he notes that modern culture is alien to the use of sacrament because technological culture is separating itself from art. As it does so creation becomes primarily human in origin and inventive rather than revelatory. It is the constant possibility for art to be propaganda for 'any real formal expression propagands the reality which caused these forms and their content to be' that makes necessary the use of sacrament. Sacrament makes obvious that 'the function of the artist is to make things *sub specie aeternitas*'. It is this interest in emphasising the necessary inadequacy of man's expression because of the dangers of technological and limited literature that indicates how much Jones learned from Chesterton.

Aside from Chesterton's close links with a group of Roman Catholic thinkers and artists, there was a large number of early twentieth century artists who were also seeing the Renaissance as the beginning of a belief in absolute human communication that could not be realised. In reaction they were turning to other modes in attempts to find a more acceptable role for art. One of the primary solutions that is reached is the concept of art creating another type of reality: one that is different from, yet analogous to, actuality. Chesterton, however, was avowedly not considering himself as a creative artist. As a result his concern with the power of this creative aspect of man has a different emphasis. Rather than searching for a new mode alone, he is out to investigate critically the consequences, with the idea that not all men will be great poets able to handle the effects. A summary of much in his artistic attitude is contained in Gilson's *Painting and Reality* which is not surprising when one thinks of their close connections to a broad stream of Thomist philosophy. In a particularly applicable section of the book which reflects Chesterton's own vocabulary, Gilson discusses the Platonic, Aristotelian and Christian effects on aesthetic theory. A brief look at the conclusion will indicate why Chesterton was so afraid of the 'creative' concept in modern art.

Whereas Platonic art is based on an imitation of an imitation, and Aristotelian on the copying of 'types', Christian art is seen purely in terms of creation, of embodying an idea. Gilson suggests that this satisfies modern artists and they turned to the 'creationist terminology' of Christian theology. Obviously contained within the definition is the possibility of a real assumption of Godhead. This Gilson rejects as not often occurring. But he himself notes not only the claim of Mallarmé, but also the anxieties of Hans Arp and Jules Bréton. The fact that Maritain and Jones even feel the need to state that man cannot create *ex nihilo* indicates their awareness of the possible interpretations of 'creativity'. Chesterton goes one step further with regard to his own artistic ideas by personally rejecting the role of the great artist, and studies many of those who attempt the role but cannot maintain the tensions it involves.

In criticising the concept of human creation in himself and others,

Chesterton recognises impressionism and rationalism as unbalanced human modes and personally develops allegory. As he does so he becomes aware of the existence of fantasy as based on human authority, and subjects the new and increasingly popular mode to an interesting examination. We have seen how close fantasy and allegory are in Chesterton's mind. They are both non-discursive and non-symbolic and therefore outside the sphere of great art. Both are based on authority; and both words are sometimes used interchangeably. However, it becomes very important for modern literature to be able to define and distinguish the two if, as Chesterton asserts, fantasy is the basis for literary technology and media distortion, while allegory is the mode not only through which the ordinary man may effectively communicate, but also through which artists can indicate the divinity that makes them great. The latter is a corollary of his belief that all great poets momentarily approach mystic art in their work in order to combine the human with the divine. Significantly, in *Chaucer* these mystic elements are seen as being developed under the guidance of St Thomas Aquinas. Aquinas introduced Aristotle into medieval Christianity and hence introduced a startling emphasis on the medium of expression. This we find reflected in Chesterton's pursuit of an adequate form. Coincident with the emphasis is another belief that Chesterton has always held: the total interrelationship of religion, morality and expression. In the light of such a belief fantasy cannot be separated from moral and ultimately religious concerns. It is a conscious attempt to impose human authority; and one must be aware of fantasy and its difference from allegory in form and intent to be able to assess the value of its propaganda.

Chesterton's approach to fantasy is primarily negative because of his personal fears that tie it into crime, insanity and sin. However, his definition of it and concern with its effects are virtually identical with Colin Manlove's conclusions in *Modern Fantasy* which is one of the few existing studies of the subject. The conclusions of Manlove's book deal with the effects of fantasy which are also Chesterton's main concern. He notes that fantasy 'reappeared' in the nineteenth century due to the Romantic idea that, 'the artist could create his own truth-systems which need have no empirical connection with our own'. As a result, 'the only basis in our reality thus became the creator not his audience'. Chesterton, while thinking that fantasy appeared with the Renaissance and grew with the advance of humanism, would agree entirely with the two corollary statements. We have seen versions of them throughout his criticism, and they happen to sum up his idea of the solipsist position.

In Manlove's conclusion the two statements lead directly to the effects of fantasy. The fantasist's 'delight in creativity' tempts him into over-contemplation of events, and an extreme self-involvement to the point of sentimentality and escapism. Chesterton made exactly this point in his analysis of 'Peter Pan'. Further, Manlove states that fantasists are 'benign determinists who do not allow evil or free will full scope'. Again we find a precise parallel in Chesterton's dislike of authorial despotism which does not allow objects or readers their own reality. The result of such effects in *Modern Fantasy*, is that fantasists are:

> often lacking in the unconscious creative imagination . . . that comes from the loss of oneself in experience and art alike. [11]

This finds its counterpart in Chesterton's emphasis on the 'unconscious' nature of the great poet, and the total self-effacement that allows one to present or indicate the identity of objects in great or mystic art.

The effects of fantasy make it a potentially perfect mode for the personal manipulation of artistic media. Yet in the five fantasies that Manlove examines, he notes that none of them actually succeed, for it is impossible to stop some elements of reality intruding. However, as Marshall McLuhan has pointed out, and as Chesterton was aware, advertising, journalism and electronic media such as films and radio can sustain the impression of false reality more effectively. There is absolutely no reason why fantasy should not be used to maintain a beneficial effect. Chesterton recognises this, and McLuhan chooses to explore the positive potential of it after writing *The Mechanical Bride*. But for Chesterton the dangers are so overwhelmingly present that he sees a personal need to avoid it completely, and finds a social role in examining it in others. The only way of ensuring the avoidance of fantasy is to use allegory. Implicit in allegory, as he defines it, is the indication of God as an external authority. The message of the medium becomes God's existence, authority and love.

In Chesterton's last major work we find him summarising and explaining the interrelationship of his religion, morality and expression through a study of his 'connatural' brother in philosophy, Thomas Aquinas. Significantly, the book approaches an assessment of the saint by way of a comparison with St Augustine. While the author is at pains to point out the positive aspects of Augustine, it becomes increasingly evident that Augustine has certain characteristics that Chesterton is anxious about. He speaks of Augustine as evolving from Platonist to Manichean to Christian; and that the association hinted of 'the danger of being *too* Platonist' in his outlook. The Augustinian tendency is linked to the predominantly 'spiritual or mystical' early medieval church. It should be noted that the word 'mystical' in this book usually refers to the purely spiritual outlook. Ultimately, the tendency is linked up with Luther who was an Augustinian monk. Chesterton sees his determinist view of Christianity as an understandable, if not inevitable corollary, to the Platonic element in Augustine.

St Thomas, by contrast, had a solid streak of reverence for material things. He stood up for the importance of the incarnation and of material reality. Chesterton goes on to define a Christian as someone who 'believes that deity or sanctity has attached to matter'. In an example that harks back to the description of a flower as indicative of life in Browning's poetry, Chesterton compares Thomas with Augustine saying:

> the Thomist begins with something solid like the taste of an apple, and afterwards deduces a divine life for the intellect; while the mystic exhausts the intellect first, and says finally that the sense of God is something like the taste of an apple. (82)

The former process is analogical, and the latter emblematic. The difference also appears in the art of Eastern and Western churches. On the one, the East has flat images or icons and it turns pictures into patterns; on the other, the West always tried for 'realistic pictures'. Eastern influence provided only abstractions however noble; they neglected the incarnation. The Western tried to portray incarnation, no matter how imperfect; their Logos was not the Word, but 'the Word made Flesh'.

As a materialist believing in the 'Word made Flesh' Thomas also believes that the whole world is analogical for the existence of God. Therefore things are not only important but they also exist. For Chesterton this is the main philosophical question: is reality real? The answer St Thomas gives is that if you cannot answer 'yes', there is really no point in even asking the question. Of course, the question is the central concern of Chesterton's early life and he adopts a similar resolution. The system St Thomas devises is seen by Chesterton as a direct follow-up of the answer. The basic concept is in the 'word *Ens*' which Chesterton finds untranslatable; but his very difficulties in conveying its meaning indicate that meaning. He observes that the English word 'being' produces a:

> different atmosphere. Atmosphere ought not to affect these absolutes of the intellect; but it does . . . The very shape and sound of words do make a difference. (179–80)

'Ens' is the absolute existence of a thing. It asserts identity not only spiritual but also material, identity which is real.

The study continues with a discussion of the idea of form in 'Thomist language'. In his definition of form the critic gives a concise basis not only for his stress on the limitations of art, but also for what he most admires in modern art. He states that form 'means actual or possessing the real decisive quality that makes a thing itself'. Matter is the 'mysterious and indefinite and featureless' element, while form is identity. Just as the sculptor knows that form is not only external appearance but the internal actuality of himself and his sculpture, so the Thomist finds form and divine identity in every object. Chesterton sees Aquinas as an artist when he is a poet, and as possessing philosophy which inspires poetry like that of Dante. St Thomas himself had 'the imagination without the imagery'. However, his prose is described as 'analogous to poetry' and 'more analogous to painting', specifically that 'produced by the *best* of modern painters, when they throw a strange and almost crude light upon stark and rectangular objects'. Chesterton allies this to the fact that painters 'deal with things without words'; they do not get misled by the common assumption that words are identities, that assumption being the basis for belief in absolute communication. The critic concludes that:

> there is no thinker who is unmistakeably thinking about things, and not being misled by the indirect influence of words, as St Thomas Aquinas. (218)

The result of such an approach is finally again compared to that of St Augustine. Aquinas concentrates on things, on form, because in contrast to the neo-Platonist mind which 'was lit entirely from within', his mind has five windows of the senses through which the light outside shines on what is within. The introspective potential of the neo-Platonists is compared to the art of St Augustine which has 'a power over words in their atmospheric and emotional aspect'. St Thomas does not possess this ability but:

> if he was without the higher uses of the mere magic of words, he was also free of that abuse of it, by mere sentimentalists of self-centred artists, which can become merely morbid and a very black magic indeed. (218)

Aquinas's method is analogical; as such it has an 'elemental and primitive poetry that shines through all his thoughts' and indicates the true relation of the mind to real things outside it. The objectivity and otherness of things provides the 'light in all poetry'. Finally he notes that 'according to Aquinas, the mind actually becomes the object. But . . . it only becomes the object and does not create the object'. The philosophy of St Thomas emphasises incarnation and material reality; his life as Chesterton portrays it shows him venerating both the physical and the spiritual. The result in his writing is in the use of analogy; and unlike Augustinianism, Thomism cannot contain the potential for fantasy either in its escapist or magical and demoniac forms, for it always indicates the existence of an external.

Etienne Gilson, the noted Thomist scholar, says that Chesterton in *St Thomas Aquinas* was 'nearer the real Thomas that I am after reading and teaching the Angelic Doctor for sixty years'.[12] That Chesterton was able to write it is an indication of how deeply St Thomas's philosophy reflects his own. The differentiation between allegory and fantasy is no crude barrier erected to keep non-believers out and believers in. Elements of individual human authority are unavoidably present in every human being, in every human system. Chesterton finds these elements within the Catholicism he has embraced, yet they do not invalidate that religion, only make it necessary to guard against their dominance. This is perhaps what he contributes most in his development of allegory. While his analogical system becomes an indication of God's existence, authority and love, it begins with a simple respect for the objects that surround one. Even though Chesterton's allegory is specifically Roman Catholic, it is Catholic in another sense. In acknowledging the external reality of the world, it disclaims the possibility of absolute human communication and stresses instead the need to search for indicative and suggestive modes to express identity. The approach, as Chesterton himself points out, is a basic modern concern.

Chesterton's fears of insanity and solipsism set him off early in pursuit of an external authority and in search of a form of identity for himself in a mode of expression. The early critical and artistic work is full of explorations for this mode, and goes hand in hand with an exploration of religious ideas. The revelation of Christianity and the idea of the mystic artist verbalising ritual, are achieved virtually simultaneously. However it is evidence both of the continuing depth of his personal unease and of his humility, that he rejected the role of artist as potentially irreligious and immoral for himself in such a humanist age. The ensuing development of the role of the mystic artist and of allegory expressed Chesterton's positive identity as one who related the divine to the human. The opposition of these concepts to fantasy and fantasists indicates his constant awareness of human weakness; and while recognising that fantasy need not have a harmful effect, he considers it extremely dangerous. Indeed contemporary discussion of the negative effects of the mode have now become second nature. Yet Chesterton went further than mere discussion of the effects to attempt a solution, however imperfect. Just as in distributism Chesterton tried to find an alternative to what he saw as the political fantasies of fascism and communism, so in allegory he tried to propose an alternative mode of communication that avoided stylistic fantasy.

The basis for Chesterton's entire attitude is found in his personal statement of philosophy, essentially a restatement of *St Thomas Aquinas*, at the end of his *Autobiography*. He himself begins with the 'pessimists' and 'hedonists' of the nineties, criticising them for their assumption of personal power. The lack of gratitude for life is a fundamental fault of their outlook. Gratitude makes necessary someone to whom to be thankful, and results in theology, acceptance of external authority and reality. Yet he also goes on to criticise those such as Bergson and Bernard Shaw who find their own personal theologies and become 'monomaniac'. There is only one theology that will satisfy him, and that is the Christian interpreted according to the incarnationist emphasis of Thomist philosophy. Having established his opponents, those who acknowledge no god or only themselves as god, Chesterton concludes by trying to state his own positive purpose, 'to serve justice'. The final image in *Autobiography* is once more of priest and poet, of 'the Builder of the Bridge, [who] is called also Claviger, the Bearer of the Key': That is, the mystic artist whose allegorical work builds a bridge between the human and divine, and in self-expression provides the analogy for the existence of God's love.

Notes

All quotations from Chesterton's works are from the editions listed in the Bibliography of Chesterton's Works, and page numbers are in brackets following extensive quotations.

All books noted are published in London unless otherwise stated.

Following is a list of abbreviations for the titles of Chesterton's books of collected essays, to facilitate reference:

Alarms and Discursions: AD
All I Survey: AS
All is Grist: AG
A Miscellany of Man: MM
As I Was Saying: AW
Avowals and Denials: ADD
Come to Think of It: CTT
Fancies versus Fads: FF
Generally Speaking: GS
G. K. C. as M. C.: GKMC
The Daily News: DN
Tremendous Trifles: TT
Uses of Diversity: UD

Chapter 1

1. *Autobiography*, p. 92.
2. These conclusions are drawn by D. Barker in *G. K. Chesterton: A Biography* (Constable, 1973), p. 50; and by C. Hollis in *The Mind of Chesterton* (Hollis and Carter, 1970), p. 28.
3. 'The Crime of Gabriel Gale', in *The Poet and the Lunatics*, p. 121.
4. Maise Ward's *Gilbert Keith Chesterton* (Sheed and Ward, 1944), p. 70.
5. O. Wilde, 'De Profundis', *The Complete Works of Oscar Wilde*, intro. V. Holland (Collins, 1971), p. 920.
6. G. B. Shaw, *The Bodley Head Bernard Shaw*, vol. I. (Max Reinhardt, The Bodley Head, 1970), p. 483.

Chapter 2

1. *DN*, 2/1/02.
2. *DN*, 4/2/02.
3. *DN*, 9/5/03.

4. *DN*, 24/8/01.
5. *DN*, 24/10/01/
6. 'Literary Picture of the Year', *The Bookman*, *XVIII* (April–September 1900), p. 80.
7. *DN*, 19/8/01.

Chapter 3

1. The Debater, Vol. I, 1891; quoted from M. Ward's *Gilbert Keith Chesterton*, p. 41.
2. *The Speaker*, 17/12/1892, p. 742.
3. Introductory to *The Wild Knight and Other Poems*, pp. 2–3.
4. E. Cammaerts, *The Poetry of Nonsense* (George Routledge & Sons Ltd., 1926).
5. E. Sewell, *The Field of Nonsense* (Chatto and Windus, 1952).
6. In *The Coloured Lands*, ed. M. Ward (Sheed and Ward, 1938).
7. *Ibid.*
8. *Ibid.*

Chapter 4

1. *TT*, p. 72.
2. 'On Lying in Bed', *TT*, p. 62.
3. 'Tom Jones and Morality', *ATC*, p. 265.
4. 'A Glimpse of My Country', *TT*, 239.
5. 'Introduction to *Nicolas Nickleby*', *ACCD*, p. 27.
6. 'Maxims of Maxim', *DN*, 25/2/05; and 'On Toys and Other Allegories', *DN*, 7/1/05, respectively.
7. *DN*, 3/2/06.
8. 'The Grave Diggers', *DN*, 26/1/07.
9. 'A Dead Poet' *ATC*, P. 278.

Chapter 6

1. *DN*, 23/9/05, and *DN*, 6/04, respectively.
2. 'The Mystagogue', *MM*, p. 96.
3. T. E. Hulme, *Speculations*, ed. H. Read (Kegan Paul, Trench, Truber & Co. Ltd., 1924), p. 184.
4. *CTT*.
5. In *The Listener*, 28/11/34, p. 921.
6. J. L. Borges, 'About Oscar Wilde', *Other Inquistions: 1937–1952* (Norwich: 1973), p. 81.
7. 'Strikes and the Spirit of Wonder', *FF*, p. 208.
8. 'Milton and Merrie England', *FF*, p. 221.

Chapter 7

1. *MM*, p. 6.
2. *A Short History of England*, p. 166.

Chapter 8

1. 'Introduction to *The Old Curiosity Shop*', *ACCD*, p. 51; and 'The Sectarian of Society', *MM*, p. 76, respectively.
2. 'Introduction to Great Expectations', *ACCD*, p. 204.
3. 'Introductory; On Gargoyles', *AD*.
4. C. S. Lewis, *The Allegory of Love* (Oxford: Clarendon Press, 1936), p. 47.
5. I. McCaffrey, *Spenser's Allegory* (Princeton: Princeton U. Press, 1976), p. 31.
6. *Ibid*, p. 80.
7. E. Vinaver, *The Rise of Romance* (Oxford: Clarendon Press, 1971), p. 101.
8. 'On Dickens and After', *CTT*, P. 231.
9. 'On the Creative and the Critical' *AS*, p. 76.
10. 'On Literary Cliques', *AS*, p. 91.
11. 'On Broadcasting', *GS*, p. 27.
12. *Sidelights*, p. 253.
13. 'On War Memorials', *AS*, p. 24.
14. 'About Loving Germans', *AW*, p. 13.
15. 'About Mad Metaphors', *AW*, p. 3.
16. *Sidelights*, p. 9.
17. 'On Blake and His Critics', *ADD*, pp. 130−1.

Chapter 9

1. 'Reading the Riddle', *DN*, 20/4/07.
2. 'On Philosophy *versus* Fiction', *AG*, p. 83.
3. 'On Absence of Mind', *DN*, 23/37.
4. *A Short History of England*, p. 77.
5. 'The introduction to *The Skeleton Key*', *GKMC*, p. 126.
6. 'On Detective Novels', *GS*, pp. 5−6.
7. 'Detective Stories', *GKMC*, pp. 168−77.
8. 'About Shockers', *AW*, p. 200.
9. 'On Humiliating Heresy', *CTT*, p. 150.

Chapter 10

1. *Autobiography*, pp. 288−9.
2. 'Wonder and the Wooden Post', *The Coloured Lands*, p. 160.
3. C. S. Lewis, *The Discarded Image* (Cambridge: Cambridge U. Press, 1967/1964), p. 119.
4. M. McLuhan and H. Parker, *Through the Vanishing Point*, (New York: Harper Colophon Books, 1969), p. 15.

5. 'The Countrymen of Mary Webb and Thomas Hardy', *The Apostle and the Wild Ducks*, ed. D. Collins (Paul Elek, 1975) p. 151.
6. Mallarmé, 'Crisis in Poetry', quoted from *The Modern Tradition*, eds. R. Ellman and C. Fieldson (New York: Oxford U. Press, 1965), p. 141.
7. S. Mallarmé, as quoted by McLuhan in 'Joyce, Mallarmé and the Press', *The Sewanee Review, Vol. LXII*, no. 1 (January—March, 1954), p. 49.
8. J. Maritain, *Creative Intuition in Art and Poetry* (The Harvill Press, 1954), p. 179.
9. W. H. Auden, 'Making, Knowing, and Judging', *The Dyer's Hand*, quoted in *The Modern Tradition*, p. 215.
10. D. Jones, *Epoch and Artist*, (Faber and Faber, 1959), p. 150.
11. C. Manlove, *Modern Fantasy: Five Studies* (Cambridge: Cambridge University Press, 1975), p. 260.
12. E. Gilson, in a letter to Father Scanell, 7 January 1966.

Bibliography

G. K. Chesterton's works consulted
Unless otherwise indicated all the books listed have been printed in
   London.

A Chesterton Calendar. 1911.
'A Crazy Tale', *The Quarto: A Volume Artistic Literary and Musical.*
   1897.
A Handful of Authors: Essays on, Books and Writers, ed. D. Collins.
   1953.
A Miscellany of Men. Beaconsfield: 1969/1912.
'A Picture of Tuesday', *The Quarto: A Volume Artistic Literary and
   musical.* 1897.
A Short History of England. 1917.
Alarms and Discursions. 1910.
All I Survey: A Book of Essays. 1932.
All is Grist: A Book of Essays. 1931.
All Things Considered. 1909.
Appreciation and Criticisms of the Works of Charles Dickens. 1911.
As I Was Saying: A Book of Essays. 1936.
Autobiography. 1936.
Avowals and Denials: A Book of Essays. 1934.
Charles Dickens, written with F. G. Kitton. 1903.
Charles Dickens. 1906.
'Charles Dickens Fifty Years Later', *Observer,* 6 June 1920.
Chaucer. 1932.
Chesterton on Shakespeare. Henley-in-Thames: 1971.
Come to Think of It: A Book of Essays. 1930.
Divorce Versus Democracy. 1916.
'Easter Sunday', *The Clarion, April 20, 1895.*
Eugenics and other Evils. 1922.
Four Faultess Felons. 1930.
Francies Versus Fads. 1923.
G. F. Watts. 1904.

G. K. C. as M. C., ed. J. P. De Fonseka. 1929.

Generally Speaking: A Book of Essays. 1928.

George Bernard Shaw. 1910.

Greybeards at Play: Literature and Art for Old Gentlemen. 1900.

Heretics. 1905.

Irish Impressions. 1919.

'Literary Pictures of the Year'. *The Bookman*, XVIII, April 1900–
    September 1900.

Magic. 1913.

Manalive. 1962/1917.

'Nothing to Shout About', *The Listener*, 28 November 1934.

Orthodoxy. Garden City: 1959/1908.

'Revolutionists and Revivalists of the 19th Century', *The Listener*, 14
    November 1934.

Robert Browning. 1903.

Robert Louis Stevenson. 1927.

St. Francis of Assissi. 1927/1923.

St. Thomas Aquinas. 1933.

Sidelights on New London and Newer York and Other Essays. 1932.

Simplicity and Tolstoy. 1912.

Tales of the Long Bow. 1925.

The Apostle and the Wild Ducks, ed. D. Collins. 1975.

The Ball and the Cross. Beaconsfield: 1963/1909.

The Ballad of St. Barbara and Other Verses. 1922.

The Ballad of the White Horse. 1911.

The Barbarism of Berlin. 1914.

The Club of Queer Trades. 1905.

The Coloured Lands. 1938.

The Crimes of England. 1915.

The Defendant. 1901.

The Everlasting Man. Garden City: 1955/1925.

The Flying Inn. 1914.

The Incredulity of Father Brown. Harmondsworth: 1976/1926.

The Innocence of Father Brown. Harmondsworth: 1975/1914.

'The Literary Portraits of G. F. Watts R. A.', *The Bookman*, XIX,
    October 1900–March 1901.

The Man Who Knew Too Much. 1961/1922.

The Man Who Was Thursday. Beaconsfield: 1963/1907.

The Napoleon of Notting Hill. 1964/1904.

The New Jerusalem. 1921.

The Paradoxes of Mr. Pond. 1937.

The Poet and the Lunatics: Episodes in the Life of Gabriel Gale. 1929.

The Return of Don Quixote. 1927.

'The Ruskin Reader', *The Academy*, June 22, 1895.

The Scandal of Father Brown. 1935.

The Secret of Father Brown. Harmondsworth: 1975/1927.

The Spice of Life and Other Essays, ed. D. Collins. Beaconsfield: 1964.

The Superstition of Divorce. 1920.

The Superstitions of the Sceptic, Cambridge: 1925.

The Thing. 1929.

The Uses of Diversity: A Book of Essays. 1921.

The Victorian Age in Literature. 1913.

The Well and The Shallows. 1935.

The Wild Knight and Other Poems. 1900.

The Wisdom of Father Brown. Harmondsworth: 1975/1914.

Tremendous Trifles. 1909.

Twelve Types. 1902.

Utopia of Usurers and Other Essays. 1917.

'Velasquez and Poussin', *The Bookman*, *XVII*, October 1899–March 1900.

'Walter De La Mare', *Fortnightly Review*, July 1932.

What's Wrong With the World. 1910.

William Blake. 1910.

William Cobbett. 1925.

Index